SO-DTC-137

DIRECTIONS IN DEVELOPMENT

Urban Environment and Infrastructure
Toward Livable Cities

Anthony G. Bigio and Bharat Dahiya

THE WORLD BANK
Washington, D.C.

Cover design by Carol Levie
Cover photos from the World Bank Photo Library.

ISBN 0-8213-5796-4

Library of Congress Cataloging-in-Publication Data

Bigio, Anthony G., b. 1951–
    Urban environment and infrastructure : toward livable cities / Anthony G. Bigio,
Bharat Dahiya.
        p. cm. — (Directions in development)
    Includes bibliographical references and index.
    ISBN 0-8213-5796-4
        1. World Bank. 2. Community development, Urban—Developing countries—
Evaluation. 3. Economic assistance—Developing countries—Evaluation.
4. Sustainable development—Developing countries. 5. Urban ecology—
Developing countries. I. Dahiya, Bharat, 1970– II. Title. III. Directions in
development (Washington, D.C.)

HN981.C6B54 2004
307.1'416'091724—dc22

                                                                    2004043534

Contents

Tables

Figures

Foreword

In the developing world and in transition economies, cities are the engines of growth, the centers of governance, and home to an increasing proportion of the national population. By 2020, urban dwellers are expected to outnumber the rural population, and cities are projected to grow significantly in size and numbers for the rest of the century, especially in Asia and Africa.

Yet the quality of life of these cities leaves much to be desired, as insufficient access to basic services—such as clean drinking water, sanitation, and solid waste disposal—cause severe health consequences for residents, and especially the poor. Pollution originating from productive activities and urban mobility also impacts negatively on human health, and natural resources in the urban areas, from the ambient air to the waterways to the soil itself, are often contaminated.

Urban pollution travels fast and wide, impacting water resources and agricultural production in the neighboring regions, and thus spreads further its negative impacts. Global emissions originating from intensive energy use in the urban areas and from fossil fuel consumption contribute to climate change. In turn, climate change exacerbates the frequency and intensity of natural disasters, many of which affect cities with increasingly high human and economic costs.

The quality of the urban environment and its linkages with regional and global sustainability are essential public goods, and as such, deserve as much attention as possible from national governments, and support from the international community. Urban environmental management, however, is also the business of local governments, which often play a key role in delivering services; of civil society, which promotes citizens' health and its rights to a clean, livable environment; and of the private sector, which can increase the efficiency and effectiveness of service delivery.

The World Bank attaches a high importance to the *expanded brown agenda*, as defined in this volume, and assists the governments of its client countries, as well as the local stakeholders, in pursuing more livable cities and an improved urban environmental quality. The Bank has an active portfolio of over US$12 billion and one-fifth of all its lending operations currently committed to the pursuit of such goals. A variety of environmentally sound interventions are needed, given the scale and the nature of the problems. Three quarters of the projects aimed at improving the urban environment are in the Water and Sanitation, Urban Development, Energy and Transport sectors, which are part of the Infrastructure Vice-Presidency.

As cities in developing countries and in transition economies continue to grow, increasing attention must be given to the quality of their urban environment and to their livability. The World Bank will continue to assist these countries in the pursuit of such goals, and this volume is a statement to our ongoing commitment.

NEMAT TALAAT SHAFIK   IAN JOHNSON
Vice-President, Infrastructure   Vice-President for Sustainable
                                             Development

Preface

This volume is an outcome of a 2002–03 research project that examined the World Bank's ongoing commitments to improving the environmental quality of cities in client countries. The project reviewed the Bank's urban environment portfolio by assessing the quantity and quality of ongoing investments aimed at improving the urban environment, the role of the various sectors involved, and the policy implications for the Bank's future work. The review was designed and carried out to fill a knowledge gap in the understanding of the Bank's commitments to improving the urban environment since the *brown agenda* became an important part of international development assistance.

The volume is intended for internal and external dissemination. The authors hope that colleagues from across the institution, both at headquarters and in the field offices, will be interested in learning more about the characteristics of the investment operations currently being implemented to improve urban environmental quality. The report should also be of interest to many Bank clients as well as to the larger development community, in particular to readers interested in urban sustainability.

The report is the first major product of the Urban Environment Thematic Group, an affiliation of World Bank staff who work on the urban environment. The group includes colleagues from many sectors, including Urban Development, Water and Sanitation, Transport, Energy, and the Environment. The Thematic Group was created in early 2002 by the Urban Development Unit to foster more cross-sector collaboration.

The Thematic Group was actively involved in the substance of the research project, and its members reviewed and discussed its findings. Ten consultation sessions and focus groups were held between June and December 2002, highlighting regional or sector aspects of the issues covered by the review.

The review's main findings were presented to a special joint session of the Urban Development, Water and Sanitation, and Environment Sector Boards (the World Bank management panels in charge of these sectors) in December 2002. There was broad endorsement for the cross-cutting approach of the research project, interest in its findings, and support for its main recommendations.

The authors hope that the report contributes to a more comprehensive understanding of the linkages between infrastructure investments and the improvement of urban environmental quality—and thus to the design of future World Bank operations in this field.

Acknowledgments

The authors wish to thank many colleagues. Maryvonne Plessis-Fraissard (Director, Transport and Urban Development Department); John Flora (former Director, Transport and Urban Development Department); Kristalina Georgieva (former Director, Environment Department); and Jamal Saghir (Director, Water and Sanitation, Energy and Mining Departments) supported this project and its main messages. Rajagopal S. Iyer, Shyamal Sarkar, Menahem Libhaber, Catherine Farvacque-Vitkovic, Dean Cira, Alexandra Ortiz, Anders Halldin, Hocine Chalal, Richard Kaguamba, Peter Johansen, Salvador Rivera, and Yan Zong, the Task Team Leaders of the 12 operations reviewed, shared valuable information and their own unique assessments of these projects. Christine Kessides (Senior Advisor, Urban Development Unit); Ede Ijjasz-Vasquez (Senior Environment Specialist, Environment Department); and Jan Janssens (Program Manager, Water and Sanitation Unit) peer-reviewed the report and provided thoughtful comments and guidance for improving it. The members of the Urban Environment Thematic Group, especially David Hanrahan (Lead Environment Specialist, South Asia Region) and Jonathan Halpern (Adviser, Water and Sanitation Unit), brought to the review the perspectives of the various sectors involved. Balakrishna Menon (Senior Urban Specialist, East Asia and Pacific Region) helped in drafting the 12 case studies. Erika Puspa (Research Assistant, Urban Development Unit) compiled the data on urban population and updated the review database. Susan Graham from the World Bank's Office of the Publisher managed the production of the book.

This research project was partially financed with a grant by DANIDA, the Danish Agency for Development Assistance, as part of its ongoing commitment to urban environmental quality in the developing world. This crucial support is gratefully acknowledged.

About the Authors

Anthony G. Bigio is a Senior Urban Specialist in the Infrastructure Department of the Middle East and North Africa Region of the World Bank. During 2002 and 2003, he served as the Coordinator of the Urban Environment Thematic Group and was based in the Urban Development Unit of the Bank. From 1999 to 2001, he was the Coordinator of the Clean Air Initiative, a global urban air quality management program. From 1994 to 1998, he was in charge of a series of capacity building programs on urban environmental management, decentralization, and social development in Sub-Saharan Africa, South Asia, and Latin America. He holds an M.A. in architecture and urban planning from the University of Rome, Italy.

Bharat Dahiya is a Consultant in the Urban Development Unit of the World Bank. Trained as an urban and regional planner, he has a PhD in urban governance and environment from the University of Cambridge. He helped implement the UN-Habitat's Sustainable Cities Program in Chennai, India. He has written World Bank policy notes on meeting the Millennium Development Goals in the urban context and addressing urban poverty. He is currently engaged in the Bank's operational work on urban development and the environment and in community-driven development projects in the Bank's East Asia and Pacific, and the Middle East and North Africa Regions.

Abbreviations

ACUACAR	Aguas de Cartagena (water and sewerage company of Cartagena)
ADB	Asian Development Bank
ASMIDAL	Entreprise Nationale des Engrais et Produits Phytosanitaires
BWSSP	Bombay Water Supply and Sewerage Projects
DGE	Direction Generale de l'Environnement
ENSIDER	Entreprise Nationale de Sidérurgie
ESCO	Energy service company (Poland)
ESMAP	Energy Sector Management Assistance Programme
FUNDACOMUN	Foundation for Community Development and Municipal Promotion
GDP	Gross domestic product
GEF	Global Environment Facility
GLE	Getlini-Eco Limited
ICR	Implementation Completion Report
IDA	International Development Agency
IDB	Inter-American Development Bank
IFC	International Finance Corporation
LUCPRO	Liaoning Urban Construction and Renewal Project Office
MCGB	Municipal Corporation of Greater Bombay
MPEC	Municipal District Heating Enterprise
NGO	Nongovernmental organization
OECD	Organisation for Economic Co-operation and Development
SIDA	Swedish International Development Agency
SINAPRED	National System for the Prevention, Mitigation and Management of Disasters (Nicaragua)
UCRESEP	Coordinating Unit for Reform of the Public Sector (Nicaragua)
UNDP	United Nations Development Programme
UPD2	Second Urban Development Project (Guinea)
URE	Energy regulatory authority (Poland)

Executive Summary

This review of the active portfolio of World Bank projects aimed at improving urban environmental quality was carried out during 2002–03 in order to assess the level of commitment of the institution to urban sustainability. The review focuses on the contributions of key sectors to urban environmental improvements, in particular on those belonging to the Infrastructure Vice-Presidency, and on how projects are contributing to achievement of the Millennium Development Goals. It also highlights some of the apparent gaps in current Bank lending in regional, spatial, and thematic terms and argues for a more comprehensive and holistic approach to urban environmental priorities, which could lead to better-integrated investments.

The Bank corporate strategy on urban development (World Bank 2000a) addresses the urban environment as part of enhancing *urban livability*. The corporate environment strategy (World Bank 2001b) states its importance through its goals of improving the quality of life, improving the quality of growth, and protecting the quality of regional and global commons. This conceptual underpinning enabled the Bank's Urban Environment Thematic Group, created in 2002, to expand the *brown agenda* identified at the 1992 Earth Summit to incorporate several new and emerging concerns. Four broad urban environmental goals were defined as the *expanded brown agenda*, drawing on both the environmental and the urban development corporate strategies:

Goal 1: Protect and enhance environmental health in urban areas.
Goal 2: Protect water, soil, and air quality in urban areas from contamination and pollution.
Goal 3: Minimize the urban impact on natural resources at the regional and global scales.
Goal 4: Prevent and mitigate the urban impacts of natural disasters and climate change.

Objectives and Methodology of the Portfolio Review

The objectives of the review were to assess the quantity and quality of ongoing investments aimed at improving the urban environment, understand the role of the various sectors involved, and assess the policy implications for the Bank's future work. Knowledge services—policy advice, technical assistance, and capacity building—were not reviewed.

The review was based on the recoding of the Bank's lending operations by sectors and themes that was instituted in fiscal 2002. It includes projects with environmental codes as well as projects that do not have such codes but whose development objectives contribute to meeting the Millennium Development Goals by reducing the proportion of people without sustainable access to safe drinking water and sanitation or by improving the lives of slum dwellers.

Basic information came from internal databases; screening of Project Appraisal Documents and Staff Appraisal Reports was done with the help of a tailor-made research instrument. This instrument captures basic project and financial data; urban environmental goals targeted; project deliverables; institutional strengthening activities; the roles of local governments, civil society, and the private sector in project design and implementation; links with the Millennium Development Goals; the size of cities in which projects are being implemented; and the monitoring and evaluation indicators being used.

Quantitative Profile of the Urban Environment Portfolio

As of March 31, 2003, 264 operations aimed at improving urban environmental quality were ongoing. In about half of these projects (48 percent), improving urban environmental quality is the primary development objective. In another 43 percent a project component addresses an urban environmental goal. Nine percent of projects include activities that addressed an urban environmental goal.

The portfolio, which includes projects approved since 1992, represents about 20 percent of the Bank's total active operations. On the basis of the relative weight of the urban environmental components in each project, the dollar value of the urban environmental investment was estimated at $12.02 billion, or 12.6 percent of the Bank's total lending commitments. However, the relatively high level of annual commitments to the urban environment appears to have declined in 2002 and 2003.

Main Findings

Urban environmental goals targeted: The vast majority of projects address issues of environmental health in urban areas (goal 1) and protecting water, soil, and air quality from contamination and pollution (goal 2). Less than a third focus on minimizing the urban impact on natural resources at the regional and global scales (goal 3). About 10 percent focus on preventing and mitigating urban impacts of natural disasters and climate change (goal 4).

Regional distribution: Projects aimed at improving urban environmental quality are being implemented in all six Bank regions. Large regional disparities are apparent, however, with investment per urban resident well below average in the South Asia Region, and above average in the Europe and Central Asia Regions, and the East Asia and Pacific Region.

Sector contributions: Many sectors are active in the urban environment portfolio, confirming that improving urban environmental quality is a shared agenda. In dollar terms, for the Bank as a whole, Water and Sanitation projects represent about 48 percent of the portfolio, followed by Urban Development (22 percent), the Environment (17 percent), and Energy (5 percent). The remainder of the portfolio includes projects from the Transport, Social Protection, Rural Development, Health, Education, Public Sector Governance, and Financial and Private Sector Development sectors. More than three-quarters of investments are managed by Sector Boards that are part of the Infrastructure Vice-Presidency.

Projects in each sector contribute to meeting the urban environmental goals in different ways:

• Water and Sanitation projects invest mainly in the provision of water supply and sanitation services; the construction of sewer lines, wastewater treatment plants, and storm water drainage systems; and to some extent improvements in water quality.
• Urban Development projects provide water supply and sanitation services and invest in sewerage and drainage infrastructure. Slum upgrading operations, solid waste management, and disaster prevention and management projects constitute other relevant urban operations.
• Environment projects mainly address waste management and reuse, including toxic and hazardous waste, treatment of effluents, and pollution management; reduction of greenhouse gas emissions; and the phasing out of ozone-depleting substances.
• Energy projects provide lending for energy efficiency, renewable sources of energy, reduction in greenhouse gas emissions, and district heating (concentrated in the Europe and Central Asia Region).
• Transport projects mainly address the abatement or prevention of vehicular emissions as part of urban mobility and often provide resources for air quality monitoring systems.

City size: In terms of number of projects, the portfolio emphasizes small cities. While about half of the urban population in the developing world lives in cities with less than 1 million people, 70 percent of the Bank's projects are concentrated there. Cities with less than 100,000 inhabitants receive 28 percent of projects, while cities with more than 5 million inhabitants receive just 10 percent of projects. Large variation is found in the spatial distribution of urban environmental projects in the Bank's regions, however, with significant investment in the megacities of East Asia.

Several factors may account for the emphasis on small cities. The institutional complexity of dealing with multiple administrative jurisdictions and the difficult nature of environmental challenges in larger urban areas could be deterring investment in megacities. The conventional understanding of the concentration of poverty in rural areas (where small urban service centers are located) and public sector policies aimed at redressing regional imbalances could be inducing investment in smaller cities, where urbanization is occurring at a faster pace than in larger cities.

Role of local counterparts: Local governments play a significant role in project design and are directly involved in implementation in 34 percent of projects. Civil society organizations appear to be involved in project design and implementation in nearly 20 percent of projects, and the private sector appears to be participating in 17 percent of operations.

Institutional strengthening: Technical assistance is concentrated on the reinforcement of sector agencies in charge of project implementation (45 percent), on capacity building (65 percent), and on technical and sector studies (34 percent). Environmental action and management plans, environmental monitoring and information systems, and environmental public education activities are supported by 22 percent of projects. Urban environmental strategies at the local level are rarely part of the technical assistance components.

Contribution to meeting the Millennium Development Goals: Projects in the urban environment portfolio appear to be contributing directly to the achievement of the Millennium Development Goals, especially to reducing maternal and child mortality (targets 5 and 6), preventing the spread of malaria and other major diseases (target 8), integrating the principles of sustainable development into country policies and programs and reversing the losses of environmental resources (target 9), improving access to safe drinking water (target 10), and fostering access to improved sanitation and security of tenure for slum dwellers (target 11).

A recent study by the Bank's Operations Evaluation Department measured livability in Bank-assisted cities against a group of comparator cities. The share of households connected to water supply and sanitation was considerably higher and the share of solid waste discarded in open dumps considerably lower in Bank-assisted cities, with positive consequences for the environmental health of the residents (World Bank 2002c). The contributions of projects are difficult to measure, however, as only two-thirds of the projects reviewed include environmental indicators. Only one-quarter include explicit environmental indicators (such as the reduction of pollution loads). The rest measure outputs rather than outcomes. Only 5 percent use quality of life indicators.

Case Studies

Twelve case studies were developed to illustrate the multisector nature of the urban environment portfolio and the integrated approach needed to address urban environmental issues (see table). The cases represent typical project deliverables found in the Bank's urban environmental work in the five main sectors (Urban Development, Environment, Water and Sanitation, Energy, and Transport) but also innovative ones. The case studies were drafted using public information for the descriptive data, the authors' subjective statements on the urban environmental aspects of the projects, and the Bank supervising Task Team Leaders' judgments on implementation progress.

Case Studies of Projects with Urban Environmental Goals

Project	Project city	Urban environmental goal	Urban environmental issues addressed
Water and Sanitation			
China: Liaoning Environment	Anshan, Dalian, Fushun, Benxi, Jinzhou	1, 2, 3	Wastewater management, clean technology
India: Bombay Sewage Disposal	Mumbai	1, 2	Sewage disposal, sanitation in slums
Colombia: Cartagena Water Supply, Sewerage, and Environmental Management	Cartagena	1, 2	Water supply and sewerage
Urban Development			
Guinea: Third Urban Development	Conakry	1, 2	Urban services, including solid waste management

Case Studies of Projects with Urban Environmental Goals

Project	Project city	Urban environmental goal	Urban environmental issues addressed
RB de Venezuela: Caracas Slum Upgrading	Caracas	1	Urban upgrading
Nicaragua: Natural Disaster Vulnerability Reduction	Secondary cities	4	Disaster management
Environment			
Latvia: Municipal Solid Waste Management	Riga	3	Solid waste management, groundwater pollution, greenhouse gas reduction
Algeria: Industrial Pollution Control	Annaba	2, 3	Industrial pollution
Kenya, Tanzania, Uganda: Lake Victoria Environmental Management	Kampala, Mwanza, Kisumu	2	Water resources and coastal zone management
Energy			
Poland: Krakow Energy Efficiency	Krakow, Skawina	3	District heating, energy efficiency
Mongolia: Improved Household Stoves in Urban Centers	Ulaanbaatar	1, 2, 3	Indoor and ambient air pollution, energy efficiency
Transport			
China: Guangzhou City Center Transport	Guangzhou	2	Air quality management

Goal 1: Protect and enhance environmental health in urban areas.
Goal 2: Protect the water, soil, and air quality in urban areas from contamination and pollution.
Goal 3: Minimize the urban impact on natural resources at the regional and global scales.
Goal 4: Prevent and mitigate the urban impacts of natural disasters and climate change.

Critical Areas and Recommendations

The review reveals a significant commitment to improving urban environmental quality. It also identifies some areas in which more may need to be done:

- The level of investment in South Asia (9 percent of total) is relatively low given the size of its urban population (20 percent of worldwide urban population) and the urban environmental challenges the region's cities are facing.
- Bank investments seem to favor smaller cities. While their urban environmental needs are important and should be met, the more complex challenges of larger urban centers and megacities, which will grow in size and number in the coming decade, will require more assistance and investments.
- Investments aimed at indoor air quality improvements are low, despite the significant contribution of poor indoor air quality to the total burden of disease worldwide. Investments in ambient urban air quality, recognized by the Bank as an important environmental priority, are also low.
- Pollution from small and medium-size enterprises and from the semi-industrial activities of the informal sector is unaddressed in the portfolio, despite its recognized impact on environmental health, including the direct effects on workers in these industries.

Some of these investment patterns may reflect the fact that Bank projects occur as the result of a dialogue with the borrowing government on its own policies and perceived priorities and those of the Bank. Bank investments cannot occur without the expressed demand from client countries. Moreover, assessing the Bank's total commitment to the urban environment—including policy advice, technical assistance, and capacity building that complement its financial support, which were not reviewed—could show a different pattern of involvement. Finally, projects that are in the pipeline may be addressing one of the review's key recommendations: that the *expanded brown agenda* be fully integrated in the Bank's lending operations. This expanded agenda would include mitigation of and adaptation to climate change, especially in coastal cities threatened by sea-level rise, assuming that client governments want to borrow for such purposes or that international grant resources are available.

A more holistic approach to meeting urban environmental challenges in a given city could be achieved if the design of sector operations were preceded by a comprehensive upstream diagnostic exercise, in which a multisector Bank team, in collaboration with client counterparts, would prepare a Rapid Urban Environmental Profile highlighting the city's priorities and the links among the different environmental challenges. This relatively low-cost effort would lay the groundwork for a more integrated selection of the issues to be addressed by Bank lending and for the preparation of higher-quality sector operations. This approach has been endorsed by the Environment, Urban Development, and Water and Sanitation Sector Boards.

I
Main Findings of the
Portfolio Review

1
Objectives of the Urban Environment Portfolio Review

This review was designed and carried out to fill a knowledge gap in the understanding of the Bank's current commitments toward improving the urban environment, commonly known as *brown agenda* issues. Partial reviews had been carried out before—as part of the Urban Development or the Environment sector portfolios, for example—but no comprehensive effort had been made to measure overall investments in Bank project activities designed to improve the urban environment. The key objectives of the research project were therefore defined as the following:

- to assess the quantity and the quality of Bank investments in improving the urban environment in the cities of its client countries
- to assess the roles of the sectors involved and their complementarities
- to make recommendations for future Bank work in this area

The portfolio review was also conceived as a vehicle to facilitate exchanges among different infrastructure sectors and between the staff of the Infrastructure and Environment networks, which share responsibility for the urban environmental agenda.

The review covers some new and emerging urban environmental issues, such as those related to the mitigation of and adaptation to climate change. It is hoped that this report will stimulate broader discussion of their importance as part of the urban environmental agenda.

The review does not and cannot provide evidence of the impact of the projects reviewed, because they are ongoing operations at different stages of implementation. Rather, the review records and interprets the projects' declared purposes at the completion of the design and approval stage.

Case studies of 12 operations provide lessons learned from their various stages of implementation. These case studies reveal the complex challenges of translating into practice the intent, objectives, and physical and institutional deliverables of these projects. Project completion will be followed by mandatory joint reporting by the Bank and the borrower and in some cases by external evaluations. None of these activities is part of the scope of work of this review.

2
The World Bank's Commitment to Improving the Quality of the Urban Environment

The World Bank's direct involvement in urban environmental management began in the early 1990s, when it contributed to the 1992 United Nations Conference on Environment and Development, also known as the Earth Summit, in Rio de Janeiro. Since then the Bank has been active in adopting the brown agenda and translating it into action. During the 1990s that agenda was defined as including all environmental externalities of human and economic activities that negatively affect human health and natural resources in and around urban areas.

Of course, many of the Bank's lending operations before 1992 focused on developmental objectives then considered to be part of the brown agenda, such as providing water supply and sanitation, upgrading slum neighborhoods, and introducing industrial pollution management. At the time, however, these activities were classified under separate sector categorizations.

Since the Earth Summit the World Bank's work in support of the urban environment has deepened and broadened in scope. The 1994 conference "The Human Face of the Urban Environment" was an important milestone, followed by the release of the *Pollution Prevention and Abatement Handbook 1998* (World Bank 1999b) and the *Greening Industry* report (World Bank 2000b).

The Bank's commitment to improving urban environmental quality can be tracked in several areas of the institution's activities. First, under the guidance of the Environmentally and Socially Sustainable Development Vice-Presidency, the Bank has placed increased importance on sustainable development throughout the institution—an emphasis that goes hand in hand with the Bank's mission of reducing poverty. Consequently, over the past 10 years, the central departments of the Infrastructure Vice-Presidency (Energy, Urban Development, Transport, and Water and Sanitation) have mainstreamed environmental sustainability and poverty reduction considerations into their corporate strategies and policy guidelines, which in turn influence the design of the Bank's projects.

Second, the Bank has given new prominence to urban environmental issues in the lending operations designed and carried out by its six regional

Vice-Presidencies. The technical work leading to the preparation and particularly implementation of Bank loans, credits, and grants contributes to improving the urban environment in the cities of the developing world. This work also increases the ability of local institutions to plan additional investments, deliver urban environmental services, and protect human health and natural resources in urban areas, especially for the poorest segments of the urban population. These lending operations are the object of the portfolio review and of this volume.

Third, in addition to lending operations that support the environment in urban areas, an integrated system of corporate safeguards applied to the design and preparation of all projects includes an environmental impact assessment to gauge, minimize, and remediate possible negative externalities of all Bank investments. The Regions are also responsible for a steady work program of analytical work that has, over the years, improved the understanding of the challenges facing the environment of specific cities of the Bank's client countries.

Fourth, the Bank's Development Economics Vice-Presidency, which is in charge of the institution's main research programs, including production of the annual *World Development Report*, has developed an important research and dissemination program on pollution management that integrates the urban environmental agenda. The World Bank Institute, the Vice-Presidency in charge of learning and capacity building, has included urban environmental training programs as part of its curriculum for nearly a decade, disseminating these programs face to face and through distance learning approaches.

In addition to these four areas of work, several regional and global programs have been created by the World Bank in partnership with UN agencies, bilateral development agencies in and governments of OECD countries, municipal governments, private companies, and civil society organizations to provide free and timely assistance to cities in developing countries. These programs support the improvement of urban environmental quality, provide technical assistance to local institutions, foster a better understanding of local challenges, and facilitate exchanges among researchers, practitioners, and policymakers in this field. Programs include the following:

- the Water and Sanitation Program, which over the past 25 years has grown to become a major international partnership providing policy advice and technical expertise on water supply and sanitation issues in developing countries
- the Urban Management Program, a global initiative started in 1989 that has generated significant innovative research on the urban governance aspects of development, including important contributions on urban environmental management

- the Energy Sector Management Assistance Programme, established in 1993, which provides grants for projects and other initiatives aimed at mainstreaming energy efficiency and the use of renewable energies and at minimizing the negative environmental externalities of energy use, particularly fossil fuel consumption
- the Metropolitan Environmental Improvement Program, established in 1994, which facilitates strategic planning exercises, in-depth analyses of major urban environmental challenges, and development of investment scenarios in major metropolitan areas in South and East Asia
- the Clean Air Initiative, a global program focused on improving urban air quality in the cities of the developing world, which has been providing technical assistance, conducting learning activities, supporting strategic planning, and disseminating knowledge in Latin America, Sub-Saharan Africa, and South and East Asia since 1998
- the Cities Alliance, created in 1999, which provides financial resources and technical assistance to help central and local governments in developing countries set up slum upgrading programs and develop city development strategies

The Urban Environment Thematic Group, an affiliation of World Bank staff, was created in early 2002 by the Urban Development Department. It includes Bank staff from many sectors, including Urban Development, Water and Sanitation, Transport, Energy, and the Environment. The group's main purpose is to ensure that the linkages between all the different streams of Bank work that relate to the urban environment—from corporate strategies to lending operations to nonlending activities—are brought to bear in a cohesive manner. The group also fosters cross-sector collaboration among the various infrastructure sectors and between the Infrastructure and the Environment networks.

The first major task of the Thematic Group was to revisit the brown agenda of the early 1990s and to adapt it to include new and emerging challenges. To do so, it turned to two key corporate strategies endorsed by the Bank's Board of Directors: the urban strategy put forth in *Cities in Transition: The World Bank Urban and Local Government Strategy* (World Bank 2000a) and the environment strategy put forth in *Making Sustainable Commitments: An Environment Strategy for the World Bank* (World Bank 2001b).

The urban strategy articulates a vision of *livable cities* as a fundamental prerequisite, together with competitiveness, good management, and financial sustainability, for successful urban development. It addresses the importance of a healthful urban environment and the need for investments in urban transport, water, and sanitation to address environmental issues with an immediate impact on human health (air pollution from lead and particulates, and waterborne diseases). It also endorses policies that promote efficiency in the use of water, energy, and waste disposal and that transfer to the polluter wherever possible the costs of negative environmental externalities. The urban strategy also recommends involvement by local governments and other local actors in participatory urban environmental management.

The environment strategy states three broad goals of the Bank's work: improving the quality of life, improving the quality of growth, and protecting the quality of the regional and global commons. Clear threats are identified in all three areas that are related to the urban environmental agenda: water-related diseases, exposure to indoor and urban air pollution and toxic wastes, the vulnerability of urban areas to natural disasters and to the local impacts of global climate change, the tradeoffs between investing in economic growth and protecting the (urban) environment, the tradeoffs between local and regional pollution abatement and taking action on global environmental change and its local impacts, and the regional and global damage to human health and natural resources caused by the spillover of pollution originating in urban areas.

Following extensive consultation, the Thematic Group formulated the following urban environmental goals:

Goal 1:   Protect and enhance environmental health in urban areas.
Goal 2:   Protect water, soil, and air quality in urban areas from contamination and pollution.
Goal 3:   Minimize the urban impact on natural resources at the regional and global scales.
Goal 4:   Prevent and mitigate the urban impacts of natural disasters and climate change.

These goals constitute the *expanded brown agenda* for the first part of the twenty-first century, framing the Bank's purpose in this area. They also constituted the basis for reviewing all active lending operations in the Bank's portfolio that contribute to the environmental quality in cities.

3
Portfolio Review Methodology

This portfolio review covers the Bank's active lending operations as of March 31, 2003 and includes Bank-executed Global Environment Facility (GEF) grants. It does not include closed operations or operations that are still under preparation nor does it include nonlending activities, such as research or the outputs of the regional and global initiatives that the Bank promotes with other partners.

The sources of information used were the Bank's Business Warehouse, an internal database containing important statistics on investment projects; Imagebank, a Web-based storehouse of information on projects and other documentation, which is accessible to the public; and the Project, Policies, and Strategies database, which details the basic features of investment projects, including their sector and theme codes. The review is based on information on project design at entry and does not include changes to project design made during implementation nor the impact of projects. The authors relied on the accuracy of the data in the institutional databases they used; they remain responsible for the analysis and interpretation of those data.

Before 2002, Bank operations were coded only by the Sector Board that had primary responsibility for implementing the investments. All Bank operations were recoded by sectors and themes in fiscal year 2002. The recoding process involved assigning sector codes based on the sector or sectors of the economy receiving Bank investments and assigning theme codes reflecting the development objectives of the operation. All active lending operations initiated since 1990 were given up to five sector codes and up to five theme codes. The year 1990 was chosen as the base year in order to measure progress toward the achievement of the Millennium Development Goals.

Table 3-1. World Bank Sector and Theme Codes Directly Relevant to the Urban Environment

Sector codes	Theme codes
Energy and Mining	*Urban Development*
LA: District heating and energy efficiency services	71: Access to urban services for the poor
LE: Renewable energy	72: Municipal finance
LZ: General energy	73: Municipal governance and institution building
Water, Sanitation, and Flood Protection	74: Other urban development
WD: Flood protection	
WA: Sanitation	*Environment and Natural Resources Management*
WS: Sewerage	
WB: Solid waste management	81: Climate change
WC: Water supply	82: Environmental policies and institutions
WZ: General water, sanitation and flood protection	84: Pollution management and environmental health
Transportation	*Social Protection and Risk Management*
TA: Roads and highways	52: Natural disaster management
TZ: General transportation	56: Other social protection and risk management

To determine which active operations could be considered as improving urban environmental quality, the authors identified the three sector and three theme codes that had direct causal links with the four urban environmental goals (table 3-1). They then created a list of project activities included as part of such operations and classified those activities in terms of the four urban environmental goals (table 3-2). In this manner, a dataset of 264 projects was culled from the Bank's 1,372 active lending operations as of March 31, 2003.

Research Instrument

Project Appraisal Documents and Staff Appraisal Reports detail the development objectives, strategic choices, project design, components and costs, safeguards, output indicators, and other relevant features of Bank projects. With the help of a tailor-made research instrument, all 264 Project Appraisal Documents and Staff Appraisal Reports were screened to cull relevant information, including information about their urban environmental features. Those features include basic project and financial data; sector and theme codes; urban environmental goals targeted; project deliverables; institutional strengthening activities; the roles of local governments, communities, and the private sector in project implementation; links with the Millennium Development Goals; the size of cities in which the projects are being implemented; and the monitoring and evaluation indicators being used. Review of each document took about one and a half hours on average.

Table 3-2. Project Activities Related to Urban Environmental Goals

Goal 1: Protect and enhance environmental health in urban areas	Goal 2: Protect water, soil, and air quality in urban areas from contamination and pollution	Goal 3: Minimize the urban impact on natural resources at the regional and global scales	Goal 4: Prevent and mitigate the urban impacts of natural disasters and climate change
Extension of water supply to unserved areas and populations	Construction and extension of trunk sewerage systems	Provision of and improvement of district heating systems	Assistance in emergency reconstruction following natural disasters (floods, cyclones, land slides, volcanic eruptions, etc.)
Provision and augmentation of city- and town-wide water supply systems	Construction and extension of trunk storm water drainage systems	Promotion of efficiency in energy generation and transmission (including efficiency improvement in thermal power plants)	Provision of support and assistance to people displaced by disasters
Provision of sanitation services, including installation of toilets	Installation of municipal wastewater, sullage, and septage collection and treatment systems	Installation of industrial effluent treatment and pretreatment plants	Formulation and promotion of disaster prevention and mitigation plans
Provision of solid waste collection services at neighborhood level	Installation of industrial liquid wastewater collection systems	Reduction of emissions of green-house gases	Construction of barriers against tidal waves and sea-level rise
Provision of access to sewerage systems at household level	Disposal and management of municipal solid waste	Phasing out of ozone-depleting substances	Consolidation of unstable slopes and vulnerable infrastructure
Construction of drains at neighborhood level	Disposal and management of hospital waste	Promotion of renewable energy sources (wind, solar, other)	

Reduction of indoor air pollution	Disposal and management of industrial and hazardous waste	Promotion of waste minimization and cleaner technologies
Reduction of noise pollution	Control and reduction of vehicular emissions	Promotion of waste reduction, reuse, recycling, and composting
	Control and reduction of industrial emissions and air pollutants	Promotion of energy efficiency in industrial and production processes
	Installation of air pollution monitoring systems	Protection of watersheds
	Promotion of nonmotorized transportation systems	Promotion of regional environmental conservation
	Promotion of efficient public transport systems	
	Conversion to and provision of cleaner fuel for automobiles	

Note: Projects often include activities related to multiple urban environmental goals.

4
Profile of the Portfolio

Two-hundred and sixty-four operations—nearly 1 out of 5 of the Bank's 1,372 active operations—are helping improve the quality of the urban environment. Total investment on the urban environment totals US$12.02 billion, or 12.6 percent of the Bank's current lending commitments as of March 31, 2003.

Trends in the Portfolio

The Bank's portfolio of active urban environmental projects spans a period of 11 years, from 1993 to 2003, based on the year of approval by the Bank's Board of Directors (figure 4-1). The small number of projects in the early years reflects the fact that older operations have closed and exited the portfolio. In contrast, the drop in the number of projects approved in 2002 and in the first three quarters of 2003 seems to point to a relative decline in investment lending related to urban environmental quality, as the total number of Bank projects approved declined in this period (from 36 in 2000 to 35 in 2001, 24 in 2002, and 9 in 2003). This decline is shared by all the sectors contributing to the urban environment portfolio, with the exception of Urban Development, which remained stable, with six new projects in 2001 and 2002.

Level of Investment in Urban Environment

Based on the level of focus on the urban environment of its development objectives and the allocation of its financial resources, each project was classified into one of three categories (figure 4-2):

- Type 1: Projects with a primarily urban environmental focus in their development objectives and in which more than 75 percent of lending is aimed at improving the quality of the urban environment
- Type 2: Projects in which one or more component addresses an urban environmental issue but whose main project focus is on other developmental goals

Figure 4-1. Active World Bank Projects Contributing to Improving the Urban Environment, 1993–2003

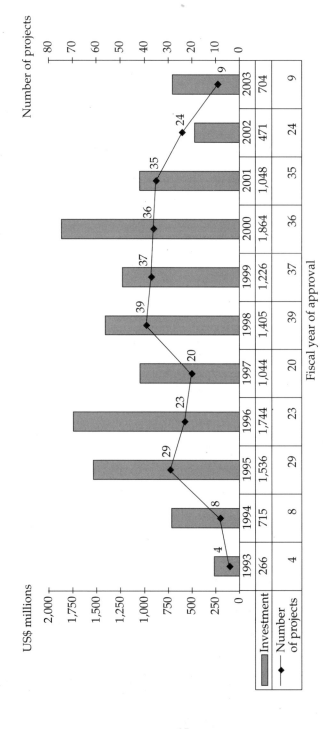

	1993	1994	1995	1996	1997	1998	1999	2000	2001	2002	2003
Investment	266	715	1,536	1,744	1,044	1,405	1,226	1,864	1,048	471	704
Number of projects	4	8	29	23	20	39	37	36	35	24	9

Fiscal year of approval

US$ millions

Number of projects

Figure 4-2. Classification of Projects by Level of Urban Environment Content

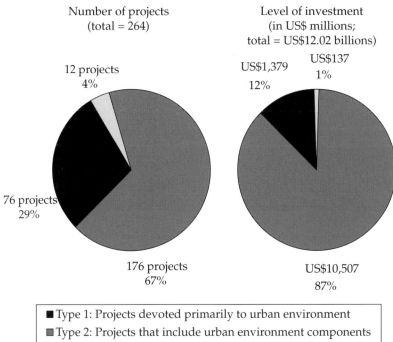

Number of projects
(total = 264)

12 projects
4%

76 projects
29%

176 projects
67%

Level of investment
(in US$ millions;
total = US$12.02 billions)

US$1,379
12%

US$137
1%

US$10,507
87%

> ■ Type 1: Projects devoted primarily to urban environment
> ■ Type 2: Projects that include urban environment components
> □ Type 3: Projects that include urban environment activities

- Type 3: Projects whose main thrust and components are not related to the urban environment but that include some activities that improve the urban environment

Regional Distribution

The East Asia and Pacific Region has the largest share of urban environmental lending, followed by Europe and Central Asia and by Latin America and the Caribbean (figure 4-3).

On average the Bank invests US$6.89 in improving urban environmental quality per urban capita (figure 4-4). The highest per urban capita investment is in Europe and Central Asia (US$8.57), where spending is almost three times as high as in South Asia (US$3.19). Investment on the urban environment per urban capita is slightly above average in Europe and Central Asia and in East Asia and Pacific; about average in Latin America and the Caribbean, the Middle East and North Africa, and Sub-Saharan

Figure 4-3. Urban Population and Investment in Improving the Urban Environment, by Region

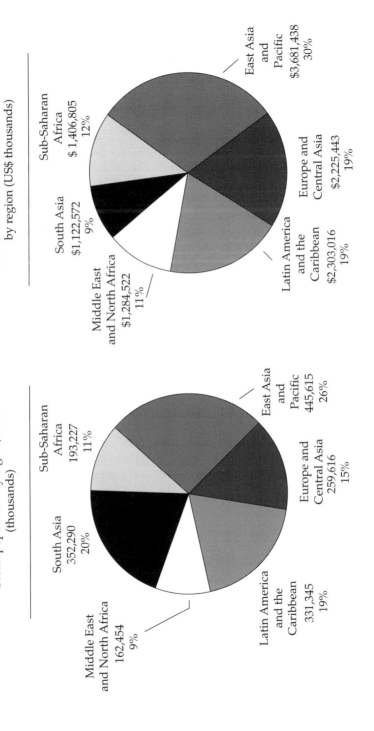

Urban population by region, 2002 (thousands)

Sub-Saharan Africa 193,227 11%

South Asia 352,290 20%

Middle East and North Africa 162,454 9%

Latin America and the Caribbean 331,345 19%

Europe and Central Asia 259,616 15%

East Asia and Pacific 445,615 26%

Investment in the urban environment by region (US$ thousands)

Sub-Saharan Africa $ 1,406,805 12%

South Asia $1,122,572 9%

Middle East and North Africa $1,284,522 11%

Latin America and the Caribbean $2,303,016 19%

Europe and Central Asia $2,225,443 19%

East Asia and Pacific $3,681,438 30%

Figure 4-4. World Bank Investment on the Urban Environment per Urban Capita, by Region

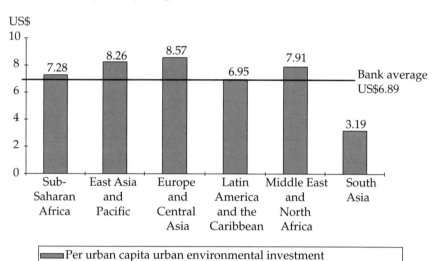

Africa; and well below average in South Asia, where 20 percent of the urban population lives but only 9 percent of investments in the urban environment are made.

These per urban capita figures do not take into account price differentials across regions, however. The same water treatment plant, for example, may cost much more in Europe and Central Asia than it does in Sub-Saharan Africa or South Asia. They also fail to reflect the fact that in some regions the Bank may be having a larger impact by promoting policy reforms or guiding the investment of national budgetary resources than it does through its lending operations. In any case, the patterns of investment reflect the priorities that client governments assign to different sectors.

Nevertheless, the need for more investment in South Asia is evident, given the levels of poverty, pollution, and environmental degradation there. A significant decline in urban lending in this region over the past decade has contributed to below-average investment on the urban environment.

Project Focus on Urban Environmental Goals

The major focus of the projects reviewed is on the provision of local environmental infrastructure and services, which contribute to the protection and enhancement of environmental health. However, several projects con-

Figure 4-5. Goals of Projects Contributing to Improving Urban Environmental Quality

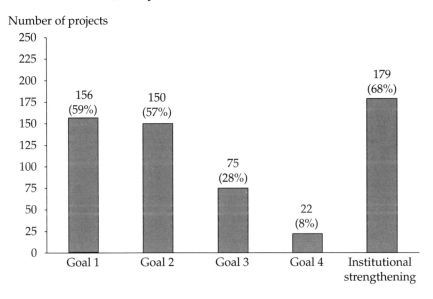

Number of projects

tribute to multiple urban environmental goals (figure 4-5). Projects aimed at providing or extending adequate primary-level waste collection services to unserved urban areas, for example, also tend to address the sustainable disposal of solid waste management, thus protecting natural resources in urban areas from contamination and pollution.

Urban Environmental Goal 1

The provision of basic environmental services is central to achieving and maintaining quality of life in urban areas. Some 156 projects (59 percent) address environmental issues at the neighborhood level, by providing primary-level infrastructure and services (such as safe water supply, sanitation, drainage, solid waste collection services, and access to sewerage systems, especially for the urban poor) and by reducing indoor air pollution and noise pollution.

Urban Environmental Goal 2

The concentration of population and economic activities in urban areas generates waste and pollution; affects the quality of natural resources (air, water, soil, and public spaces); and leads, in the absence of adequate infrastructure and services, to the deterioration of living conditions. Some 150 projects (57 percent) provide infrastructure and services in pollution control and waste management, environmental monitoring, and other environmental services.

Urban Environmental Goal 3

The concentration of population and economic activities in urban areas also affects natural resources at the regional and global scales. The discharge of untreated industrial effluents, for example, pollutes rivers downstream; the use of coal in district heating systems has regional and global impacts. To minimize these impacts, 75 projects (28 percent) provide for energy conservation and efficiency (in generation, transmission, and use); improved district heating systems; collection and treatment of liquid industrial effluents; reduction of greenhouse gases and ozone-depleting substances; promotion of renewable energy; waste minimization; and watershed protection and management.

Urban Environmental Goal 4

Urban areas across the world are affected by a growing number of natural disasters of increasing intensity and cost (see Walter 2002 and Bigio 2003). Cities and towns are also susceptible to the interrelated impacts of climate change and the rise in sea level caused by global warming. Some 22 projects (8 percent) support activities aimed at preventing and mitigating the urban impacts of natural disasters and climate change. These activities include emergency reconstruction, disaster prevention measures and plans, construction of barriers against sea waves and the rise in sea level, and consolidation of unstable slopes and vulnerable infrastructure.

Institutional Strengthening and Technical Assistance

Addressing urban environmental issues demands appropriate institutional structures; strategic and sector planning; policy formulation and reform; environmental tools and methods (action management plans, audits, monitoring and information systems, and education and awareness campaigns); support to civil society; private sector development; and capacity building. The fact that urban environmental issues are addressed by many sectors adds complexity and heightens the need for addressing these institutional and capacity issues through development projects. Some 179 projects (68 percent) aim to strengthen institutions and build capacity.

The urban environmental goals of each project are correlated with the level of urban environmental content (table 4-1). Among projects devoted primarily to improving the urban environment (type 1), for example, the highest percentage of projects focus on urban environmental goal 3.

Table 4-1. Projects by Urban Environmental Goal and Level of Urban Environmental Content

Urban environmental goal	Type 1 (primarily urban environmental)	Type 2 (includes urban environmental components)	Type 3 (includes urban environmental activities)	Total Bank-wide
Goal 1: Protect and enhance environmental health in urban areas	108 (69%)	39 (25%)	9 (6%)	156 (100%)
Goal 2: Protect water, soil, and air quality in urban areas from contamination and pollution	103 (69%)	43 (29%)	4 (3%)	150 (100%)
Goal 3: Minimize urban impact on natural resources at regional and global scales	65 (87%)	9 (12%)	1 (1%)	75 (100%)
Goal 4: Prevent and mitigate urban impacts of natural disasters and climate change	14 (64%)	7 (32%)	1 (5%)	22 (100%)

5
Sector Contributions to the Portfolio

The cross-sectoral nature of urban environmental issues and the integrated approach needed to address them are reflected in the sector composition of the Bank's urban environment portfolio. The urban environmental agenda is shared by many sectors, including Water and Sanitation, Urban Development, Energy, Transport, and the Environment (figure 5-1). Rural development, social protection, private sector development, education, health, public sector governance, and the financial sector also contribute to this portfolio, albeit marginally.

More than three-quarters (79 percent) of urban environmental investment is contributed by the Infrastructure Vice-Presidency (Water and Sanitation, Urban Development, Energy, and Transport), with almost half (48 percent) of all investment in the Water and Sanitation sector.

Investments in the Water and Sanitation, Urban Development, and Environment sectors are larger than the average urban environmental investment, because most of these projects are primarily type 1 projects (table 5-1). The average urban environmental investment per project in the Water and Sanitation (US$67.4 million) and Urban Development (US$47.3 million) sectors is larger than the average Bank investment in the urban environment (US$45.5 million). In contrast, Energy sector projects tend to be much smaller than average (US$26.8 million). Transport sector projects are also smaller than average (US$10.3 million), as most are type 2 or type 3 projects.

In the five main sectors, urban environmental projects represent 44 percent of all active projects (table 5-2). These investments account for just one-fourth of total commitments, however. The level of investment varies across sectors. In the water supply and sanitation sector, 63 percent of projects and 96 percent of commitments are part of the urban environment portfolio, given the "lumpiness" of these investments. In the other main sectors, the percentage of urban environmental investments is smaller than the percentage of projects.

Figure 5-1. Number of Urban Environmental Projects and Level of Investment, by Sector

Number of urban environmental projects

Water and sanitation 85 (32%)
Rural development 4 (2%)
Other 12 (5%)
Social protection 12 (5%)
Transportation 23 (9%)
Energy 23 (9%)
Environment 45 (17%)
Urban development 60 (23%)

Level of investment (US$ millions)

Social protection $151 (1%)
Other $134 (1%)
Transportation $237 (2%)
Rural development $409 (3%)
Energy $617 (5%)
Environment $1,912 (16%)
Water and sanitation $5,727 (48%)
Urban development $2,836 (24%)

Table 5-1. Projects by Sector and Level of Urban Environmental Content
(number of projects, except where otherwise indicated)

Sector	Average urban environmental investment in project ($US millions)	Type 1 (primarily urban environmental)	Type 2 (includes urban environmental components)	Type 3 (includes urban environmental activities)	Number of projects
Water and Sanitation	67.4	79	6	0	85
Urban Development	47.3	35	22	3	60
Environment	42.5	40	5	0	45
Energy	26.8	17	5	1	23
Transport	10.3	1	20	2	23
Other sectors	24.8	4	18	6	28
Bank-wide	45.5	176	76	12	264

Table 5-2. Number of Projects and Level of Urban Environmental Investment, by Sector

Sector	Total number of projects in the sector	Total commitments under the sector (US$ millions)	Number of urban environmental projects	Urban environmental investment (US$ millions)	Percentage of urban environmental projects	Percentage of urban environmental investment
Water and Sanitation	96	5,979	60	5,727	63	96
Urban Development	70	5,062	60	2,836	86	56
Environment	61	2,792	45	1,912	74	68
Energy	89	9,030	23	617	26	7
Transport	159	18,589	23	237	14	1
Total	475	41,452	211	11,329	44	27

Table 5-3. Distribution of Urban Environmental Investment across Bank Regions

(percent)

Sector	Sub-Saharan Africa	East Asia and Pacific	Europe and Central Asia	Latin America and the Caribbean	Middle East and North Africa	South Asia	Bank-wide
Water and Sanitation	49	57	20	52	53	55	48
Urban Development	34	10	40	17	31	28	24
Environment	2	17	15	26	14	13	16
Energy	5	1	21	*	*	2	5
Transport	6	2	0	2	*	2	2
Other	3	13	3	3	2	*	6

* Less than 1 percent.

Regional Distribution of Urban Environmental Investment

Water and Sanitation represents the largest share of regional urban environmental investment in East Asia and Pacific, and the smallest share in Europe and Central Asia (table 5-3). Urban Development represents the largest share in Europe and Central Asia and the smallest share in East Asia and Pacific. Environment represents the largest share in Latin America and the Caribbean and the smallest share in Sub-Saharan Africa. Energy has the largest share in Europe and Central Asia and the smallest share in Latin America and the Caribbean and in the Middle East and North Africa. Transport has the largest share in Sub-Saharan Africa and the smallest share in Europe and Central Asia, where no projects are in place. Other sectors contribute 5.8 percent of total urban environmental investment across the regions.

Sector Contribution to Urban Environmental Goals

While most projects under review target urban environmental goals 1 and 2, the picture varies across sectors (table 5-4). Water and Sanitation and Urban Development projects concentrate on urban environmental goals 1 and 2, Environment projects contribute mainly to goals 2 and 3, Energy projects focus on goal 3, and Transport projects focus on goal 2.

Table 5-4. Urban Environmental Goals Addressed, by Sector
(percent)

Urban environmental goal	Water and Sanitation	Urban	Environment	Energy	Transport	Other	Bank-wide
Goal 1: Protect and enhance environmental health in urban areas	87	72	20	17	26	71	59
Goal 2: Protect water, soil, and air quality in urban areas from contamination and pollution	68	60	56	22	65	39	57
Goal 3: Minimize the urban impact on natural resources at regional and global scales	16	7	71	87	9	11	28
Goal 4: Prevent and mitigate urban impacts of natural disasters and climate change	5	17	2	0	17	11	8
Total number of projects	85	60	45	23	23	28	264

Water and Sanitation

Water and Sanitation projects constitute the largest share of operations in the active urban environment portfolio, with 85 projects and 48 percent of urban environmental investment (figure 5-2). Of these projects, 93 percent are classified as type 1 projects (that is, the project is primarily devoted to improving the urban environment).

Water and Sanitation investments are significant in all six Bank regions. Investment is largest in East Asia and Pacific, where active commitments exceed US$2 billion. These investments represent the single largest cohort of investments reviewed. Water and Sanitation operations focus largely on achieving urban environmental goals 1 and 2, with some projects contributing to the attainment of goal 3.

More than half of the projects reviewed include components on augmenting water supply (63 projects), municipal wastewater treatment (56

Figure 5-2. Urban Environmental Projects in the Water and Sanitation Sector, by Region

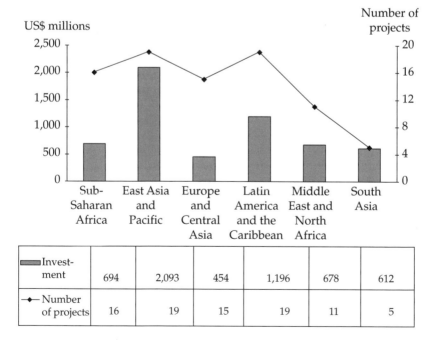

	Sub-Saharan Africa	East Asia and Pacific	Europe and Central Asia	Latin America and the Caribbean	Middle East and North Africa	South Asia
Invest-ment	694	2,093	454	1,196	678	612
Number of projects	16	19	15	19	11	5

projects), extending water supply (43 projects), or constructing or extending trunk sewerage systems (43 projects). More than a quarter of the projects reviewed include components on providing access to sewerage systems (27 projects) or sanitation (22 projects).

These numbers reveal the focus of Water and Sanitation investments on providing trunk infrastructure for the supply of clean drinking water and the disposal and treatment of wastewater. Bank investments are also targeting expansion of service provision, by augmenting water supply, improving sanitation, and increasing the number of connections to sewerage lines.

Nine projects provide water quality monitoring, more than half of them in East Asia and Pacific. Components of these projects overlap with components of projects in the Environment sector. Nine other projects introduce water conservation measures. Four of these projects are in the Middle East and North Africa.

Ten Water and Sanitation projects provide solid waste collection and eight provide solid waste disposal and management, establishing important linkages between different aspects of environmental services delivery. Nine of the solid waste collection and seven of the solid waste disposal and management projects are in East Asia and Pacific. Four other projects in that region focus on waste minimization and the use of clean technologies. All three projects that are providing waste reuse and recycling are in the Middle East and North Africa, as are the two projects providing efficiency in energy generation related to water supply. Seven projects provide trunk storm-water drainage infrastructure, another important aspect of citywide environmental management, four of which are in East Asia and Pacific. Eight projects provide industrial effluents treatment, six of which are in East Asia and Pacific.

Three case studies exemplify Water and Sanitation sector projects aimed at improving urban environmental quality. The Liaoning Environment Project (China) aims to protect the water resources of Liaoning Province, while improving environmental protection, water pollution control, and wastewater and solid waste management and introducing air pollution control and cultural assets management. The Bombay Sewage Disposal Project (India) focuses on enhancing the provision of sewerage services, by introducing direct charges to beneficiaries, and on improving the health and environmental conditions in the metropolitan area, including those of slum dwellers. The Cartagena Water Supply, Sewerage, and Environmental Management Project (Colombia) aims to improve water and sewerage services and the sanitary conditions of the city's poorest people, facilitate the environmental clean-up of water bodies surrounding the city, and improve the sustainability of water and sanitation services through increased private sector participation.

Urban Development

Urban Development projects constitute the second-largest share of operations in the active urban environment portfolio, with 60 projects and 24 percent of total urban environmental investments (figure 5-3). Only 58 percent of the Urban Development projects reviewed are classified as primarily urban environment (type 1) investments. Some 37 percent of the projects reviewed have urban environment components (type 2); 5 percent include some urban environmental activities (type 3).

Urban Development investments are present in all six Bank regions. Investment is largest in Europe and Central Asia, where active commitments total almost US$900 million. Operations focus largely on achieving urban environmental goals 1 and 2. Several projects target goal 4.

More than one-third of the projects reviewed include components on extending water supply (27 projects), collecting solid waste (24 projects), providing sanitation (23 projects), improving trunk storm-water drainage (23 projects), disposing of and managing solid waste (21 projects), and

Figure 5-3. Urban Environmental Projects in the Urban Development Sector, by Region

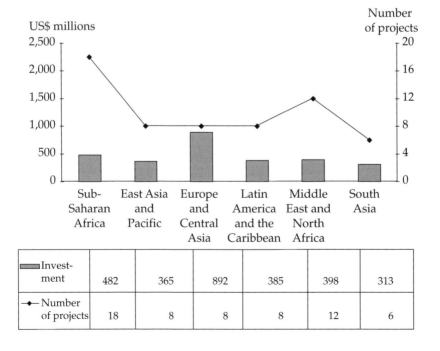

	Sub-Saharan Africa	East Asia and Pacific	Europe and Central Asia	Latin America and the Caribbean	Middle East and North Africa	South Asia
Investment	482	365	892	385	398	313
Number of projects	18	8	8	8	12	6

building drains and drainage networks (20 projects). More than a quarter of the projects reviewed include components on augmenting water supply (18 projects), constructing trunk sewerage systems (17 projects), improving municipal wastewater treatment (16 projects), and providing access to sewerage systems (15 projects).

These numbers confirm the focus of Urban Development operations on providing basic urban environmental services, with priority given to secondary and tertiary infrastructure networks for water and sanitation. These priorities coincide with the sector's policy focus on low-income informal settlements and slum upgrading. Six operations finance erosion control works and are related to stabilizing such neighborhoods. A significant number of investments are also being made in trunk infrastructure and wastewater treatment plants.

Many projects provide solid waste collection, usually including investments in solid waste disposal and management (sanitary landfills). Three projects in East Asia and Pacific support waste reuse and recycling, and three finance hazardous waste management. Solid waste management appears to be fully shared between the Urban Development and Environment sectors.

Of significance are the 10 operations providing disaster mitigation measures. The two loans to Turkey in this area represent 20 percent of active commitments for Urban Development in this portfolio and account for the disproportionate share of investments going to Europe and Central Asia. Four of the 10 disaster mitigation operations are in this region. Related operations include seven projects that provide disaster prevention plans, three of which are in Europe and Central Asia, and three projects that finance emergency reconstruction, also in Europe and Central Asia. In addition to the projects provided under Energy sector management, four district heating projects, three of which are in Europe and Central Asia, are also being implemented under the Urban Development sector.

Three case studies exemplify Urban Development sector projects aimed at improving urban environmental quality. The Third Urban Development Project (Guinea) aims to improve living conditions in Guinea's capital, Conakry, by providing basic services, including solid waste management, and supporting priority investments in other major urban centers. The Caracas Slum-Upgrading Project (República Bolivariana de Venezuela) aims to improve the quality of life of several informal settlements in the metropolitan area by financing community driven, sustainable, and replicable infrastructure improvements. The Natural Disaster Vulnerability Reduction Project (Nicaragua) aims to strengthen institutional capacity in disaster management and mitigation, promote awareness and disaster preparedness, and implement vulnerability reduction and mitigation measures at the local level.

Environment

Environment projects constitute the third-largest share of operations in the active urban environment portfolio, with 45 projects and 17 percent of total urban environmental investments (figure 5-4). Some 89 percent of these projects are classified as primarily urban environment investments (type 1). The remaining 11 percent of projects reviewed have urban environment components (type 2).

Environment investments are present in all six Bank regions. Investment is largest in East Asia and Pacific, where active commitments total more than US$600 million. Most operations target urban environmental goals 2 and 3.

More than a quarter of the projects reviewed include components on solid waste disposal and management (16 projects) and the phasing out of ozone-depleting substances (14 projects). More than a fifth of projects include components on industrial and hazardous waste management (11 projects) and waste reuse and recycling (9 projects). These numbers confirm the sector's focus on managing pollution at the urban, regional, and global levels.

Figure 5-4. Urban Environmental Projects in the Environment Sector, by Region

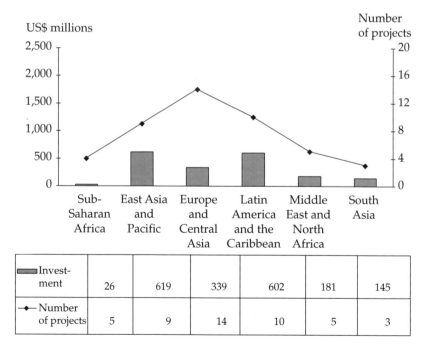

	Sub-Saharan Africa	East Asia and Pacific	Europe and Central Asia	Latin America and the Caribbean	Middle East and North Africa	South Asia
Investment	26	619	339	602	181	145
Number of projects	5	9	14	10	5	3

Solid waste disposal and management (sanitary landfills) and solid waste collection are projects the sector shares with Urban Development. The largest share of these investments is concentrated in Europe and Central Asia. The Bank is also supporting a regional program in the Caribbean Community countries.

In protecting urban soil from contamination and pollution, projects in the Environment sector emphasize industrial and hazardous waste management and waste reuse and recycling. Five projects address hospital waste management; another six address waste minimization and the introduction of cleaner technologies in industrial production cycles.

The phasing out of ozone-depleting substances is intended to protect the quality of the global commons. (These projects are included in the urban environment portfolio because urban areas are where ozone-depleting substances are produced and consumed in the highest concentrations.) Six of the 14 projects are in East Asia and Pacific. Six projects, four of which are in Europe and Central Asia, reduce greenhouse gas emissions.

Environment projects address water resource management through operations aimed at regulating urban usage of groundwater (eight projects, seven of which are in Europe and Central Asia); improving water quality monitoring (four projects, three of which are in Latin America and the Caribbean); treating industrial effluents (six projects); and building municipal wastewater treatment plants (four projects). Four projects address air pollution and air quality monitoring, and six address the control of vehicular emissions, an area shared with the Transport sector.

Three case studies exemplify Environment sector projects aimed at improving urban environmental quality. The Municipal Solid Waste Management Project (Latvia) aims to introduce modern, self-sustaining solid waste management through the maximum sequestration of methane generated from landfills, thereby reducing greenhouse gas emissions and creating a revenue stream to cover capital and operational costs. The Industrial Pollution Control Project (Algeria) aims to reduce exposure to hazardous pollution that causes health problems and serious ecological degradation by investing in the industrial sector in Annaba and strengthening the institutional and legal framework. The Lake Victoria Environmental Management Project (Kenya, Tanzania, and Uganda) aims to restore the natural ecosystem of Lake Victoria, which is threatened by urban effluents, rural runoff, and overuse of fisheries. The project seeks to benefit riparian communities and conserve biodiversity.

Energy

Energy projects constitute the fourth-largest share of operations in the active urban environment portfolio, with 23 projects and 5 percent of total urban

environmental investments (figure 5-5). Some 74 percent of the Energy projects reviewed are classified as primarily urban environment investments
(type 1). Another 22 percent have urban environment components (type
2). Four percent of the projects reviewed include some urban environmental
activities (type 3).

Energy investments are present in all six Bank Regions. Investment is
largest in the Europe and Central Asia Region, with active commitments
of almost US$470 million. Most environmental operations target urban
environmental goal 3.

More than half of the projects reviewed include a component on increasing efficiency in energy generation (12 projects). More than one-quarter
include components on district heating systems (eight projects), greenhouse gas abatement (seven projects), or promotion of renewable energy
(seven projects).

Figure 5-5. Urban Environmental Projects in the Energy Sector, by Region

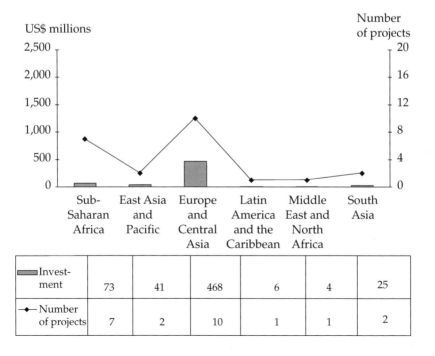

	Sub-Saharan Africa	East Asia and Pacific	Europe and Central Asia	Latin America and the Caribbean	Middle East and North Africa	South Asia
▬ Invest-ment	73	41	468	6	4	25
◆ Number of projects	7	2	10	1	1	2

Operations addressing efficiency in energy generation are generally the same projects that are providing district heating systems, often by introducing heat and electricity cogeneration plants. All of the district heating projects are in Europe and Central Asia, as are 10 out of the 12 energy efficiency operations. These investments often reduce gas emissions and promote renewable energy use. Three of these projects also monitor air pollution and air quality.

Three Energy operations in Sub-Saharan Africa are promoting the use of renewable energy for extending and augmenting water supply and providing sanitation in urban locations not adequately served by the electricity distribution grid.

Two case studies exemplify Energy sector projects aimed at improving urban environmental quality. The Krakow Energy Efficiency Project (Poland) aims to improve the energy efficiency of municipal heating systems, decrease heat energy consumption at the end-user level, and develop the knowledge and mechanisms for private sector financing of energy efficiency schemes. The Improved Household Stoves in Urban Centers Project (Mongolia) aims to reduce coal fuel consumption in the traditional housing areas (*ger* areas) of Ulaanbaatar by introducing efficient indoor stoves, thereby decreasing indoor air pollution and its impacts on human health as well as carbon dioxide emissions originating from coal burning.

Transport

Transport projects constitute the fifth-largest share of operations in the active urban environment portfolio, with 23 projects and 2 percent of total urban environmental investments (figure 5-6). Only 4 percent of the projects reviewed are classified as primarily urban environment investments (type 1). Some 87 percent of the Transport projects reviewed have urban environment components but a main focus on other sector objectives (type 2). Nine percent of the projects include some urban environmental activities (type 3).

Transport investments are present in five of the six Bank regions (every region except Europe and Central Asia). Investment is largest in the Sub-Saharan Africa Region, where active commitments total almost US$90 million. Most Transport operations target urban environmental goal 2.

More than one-third of the projects reviewed include components on controlling vehicular emissions (nine projects) or monitoring air pollution and air quality (nine projects). More than one-quarter of the projects include components on efficient public transport systems (five projects), promotion of cleaner fuels for vehicles (six projects), and reduction in noise pollution (six projects). The four projects in East Asia and Pacific that address the control of vehicular emissions are also providing efficient public trans-

Figure 5-6. Urban Environmental Projects in the Transport Sector, by Region

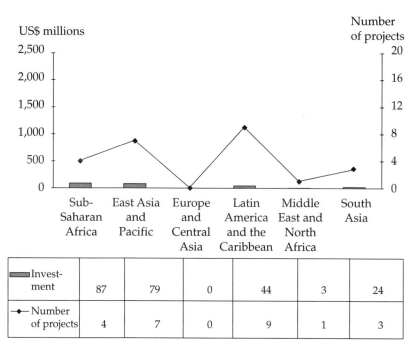

	Sub-Saharan Africa	East Asia and Pacific	Europe and Central Asia	Latin America and the Caribbean	Middle East and North Africa	South Asia
▬ Invest-ment	87	79	0	44	3	24
◆ Number of projects	4	7	0	9	1	3

port systems and introducing cleaner fuels for vehicles. The four projects in Latin America and the Caribbean addressing the control of vehicular emissions are also providing noise pollution reduction and monitoring air pollution and air quality.

One case study illustrates a Transport sector project aimed at improving urban environmental quality. The Guangzhou City Center Transport Project (China) aims to improve the accessibility of the city center of Guangzhou by promoting the efficient use of the urban transport system in an environmentally sustainable way.

6
Urban Environmental Investments in Small and Large Cities

City Size and Urban Environmental Issues

The size of the population of an urban agglomeration and the nature of the urban environmental problems it faces are strongly correlated. Typically, large cities face issues of industrial pollution, congestion, and deteriorating air quality, which smaller centers do not experience. In contrast, smaller centers may still be facing fundamental issues of water supply, sanitation, and solid waste management, which larger cities may be providing.

In larger urban areas, intraurban differentials in service provision are relevant, typically between wealthier central areas and informal neighborhoods. The nature of urban environmental problems is also influenced by such factors as geographic location, climatic considerations, and levels of socioeconomic development. Population size nevertheless remains a good indicator of the type of urban environmental issues a city may be facing.

City Size and Urban Environmental Projects

To assess the spatial focus of urban environmental investments, the study analyzed the distribution of projects in relation to the size of the population of the urban centers in which they are being implemented (figure 6-1). Urban population data for the year 2002 for each of the Bank's client countries were aggregated and classified by the six city size categories used by UN-Habitat (under 100,000; 100,000–500,000; 500,000–1 million; 1–5 million; 5–10 million; and over 10 million). This national information was then aggregated to obtain the total urban population in each of the six Bank regions and analyzed to assess the projects' focus on cities of different sizes. It is important to note that the population of larger cities (with multiple jurisdictions) includes the inhabitants of the core city as well as those of the surrounding cities and towns; the total number of inhabitants comprise the metropolitan area/urban agglomeration of that core city. This metropolitan area/urban agglomeration designation applies specifically, but not exclusively, to cities with more than 1 million people.

Figure 6-1. Number of Urban Environmental Projects, by City Size

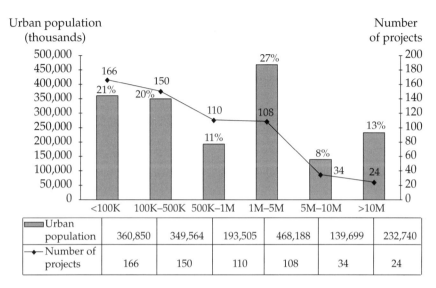

	<100K	100K–500K	500K–1M	1M–5M	5M–10M	>10M
Urban population	360,850	349,564	193,505	468,188	139,699	232,740
Number of projects	166	150	110	108	34	24

Note: Because some projects invest in cities of different size, the number of projects exceeds 264.

The analysis shows that while about half of the developing world's urban population lives in cities with fewer than 1 million inhabitants, 72 percent of the Bank's urban environmental projects are concentrated there. This relative emphasis on smaller urban centers is particularly acute at both ends of the spectrum. The smallest urban centers—cities with fewer than 100,000 inhabitants, which account for 21 percent of the total urban population— benefit from 28 percent of the Bank's projects; the largest urban centers—cities with more than 5 million inhabitants, which account for 21 percent of the total urban population—benefit from 10 percent of the projects.

The information available on these operations made it possible to establish only the number of projects active in cities of different sizes, not the volume of investment. A more detailed review of urban environmental investments by city size might contradict—or reinforce—the correlations described here.

Regional Variations

The definition of a large urban center varies across regions. A large city in Europe and Central Asia, for example, would be considered a small or

Table 6-1. Number of Urban Environmental Projects, by City Size and Region

Region	<100K	100K–500K	500K–1M	1M–5M	5M–10M	>10M	Total projects
East Asia and the Pacific	20	28	22	28	10	11	50
Europe and Central Asia	34	27	16	20	4	1	53
Latin America and the Caribbean	37	31	25	28	9	4	53
Middle East and North Africa	24	23	17	9	2	0	35
South Asia	12	10	9	9	8	8	19
Sub-Saharan Africa	39	31	21	14	1	0	54
Bank-wide	166	150	110	108	34	24	264

Note: Number of projects exceeds 264 because some projects invest in cities of different sizes.

medium-size city in Asia, and it would experience very different urban environmental problems. Moreover, larger cities in Asia and Africa are experiencing more rapid population growth, because of higher natural birth rates and rural-urban migration rates than their counterparts in other regions, where urbanization is tapering off. As a result, gaps in infrastructure and service provision are greater in these cities, leading to more urban environmental problems.

The regional analysis of urban environmental investments by city size confirms the general Bank-wide picture, with some significant variations (table 6-1). Most of the projects in cities with 1–5 million people are in East Asia and Pacific, Latin America and the Caribbean, and Europe and Central Asia. East Asia and Pacific, Latin America and the Caribbean, and South Asia stand out in terms of number of projects in large cities (5–10 million inhabitants) and megacities (more than 10 million inhabitants). East Asia and Pacific has the smallest number of projects in cities with less than 100,000 inhabitants.

Urban Environmental Goals and City Size

The pattern of concentrating on cities with fewer than 1 million people is reflected in the distribution of projects by urban environmental goal. All four urban environmental goals are represented equally in proportion to their relative weight in the portfolio (table 6-2). In cities with more

Table 6-2. Number of Urban Environmental Projects, by Goal and City Size

Urban environmental goal	<100K	100K–500K	500K–1M	1M–5M	5M–10M	>10M	Total projects
Goal 1: Protect and enhance environmental health in urban areas	101	90	61	53	6	6	156
Goal 2: Protect water, soil, and air quality in urban areas from contamination and pollution	85	81	62	56	14	11	150
Goal 3: Minimize the urban impact on natural resources at regional and global scales	46	43	36	40	14	15	75
Goal 4: Prevent and mitigate urban impacts of natural disasters and climate change	15	12	7	8	4	0	22

Note: Number of projects exceeds 264 because some projects invest in cities of different sizes.

than 1 million inhabitants, a larger percentage of projects target goal 2 than other goals. Goal 4 is pursued more in smaller urban centers than in larger ones, presumably because of the prevalence of natural disaster mitigation and reconstruction activities; no project is pursuing goal 4 in a megacity.

Sector Focus on City Size

Cities with fewer than 500,000 inhabitants attract the bulk of the Water and Sanitation, Urban Development, and Energy sector investments, which focus on providing neighborhood-level and citywide infrastructure and services (table 6-3). Transport sector operations are prevalent in cities with 1–5 million inhabitants, where issues of air pollution and public transport are very important. Environment sector operations dominate in large cities and megacities.

City Size and Urban Environmental Focus

Interpreting this pattern of urban environmental investments across urban centers of different size is tricky. The following reasons can nevertheless be put forth:

1. In larger countries (for instance, Brazil or China), government policies may tend to favor investments in small or medium-size cities, which are considered poorer than larger ones. Larger cities are thought to have more resources and capacity to invest in infrastructure and services—and in turn to address their urban environmental issues—because of their stronger economies and proximity to national political centers of power.

2. The urban environmental problems of smaller cities are generally less complex and smaller in scale than those in larger cities, and could be addressed with a preventive approach. Hence it may be easier to achieve results in smaller cities than in larger ones.

3. Investing in larger cities, where environmental problems often span urban and regional space, involves working with multijurisdictional institutional settings. This adds significant complexity to the challenge of addressing urban environmental problems, and it increases the cost of investments, including the transaction costs associated with defining and forming consensus around urban environmental priorities. The often differing agendas of separate municipalities within the same metropolitan area, problems of administrative separatism, and the greater sharing of responsibilities among stakeholders in larger cities require strategic integration in urban environmental planning and management (Bartone and others 1994; Dahiya and Pugh 2000).

Table 6-3. Number of Urban Environmental Projects, by Sector and City Size

Sector	<100K	100K–500K	500K–1M	1M–5M	5M–10M	>10M	Total projects
Water and Sanitation	54	52	41	31	7	5	85
Urban Development	70	68	38	43	12	3	60
Environment	67	67	56	56	24	31	45
Energy	78	48	43	43	9	9	23
Transport	26	30	17	57	17	4	23
Other	24	17	13	8	4	1	28
Bank-wide	166	150	110	108	34	24	264

Note: Number of projects exceeds 264 because some projects invest in cities of different sizes.

7
The Role of Local Government, Civil Society, and the Private Sector

Urban environmental management relies on the comparative advantages of various agencies and stakeholders from the public and private sectors as well as on civil society organizations in different local contexts. However, the Bank lends to national governments, and therefore, government agencies generally implement projects. Eighty-seven percent of the projects reviewed are being implemented by government agencies. In a small proportion of projects (13 percent), government agencies are also involved in identifying subprojects (targeting actions to specific communities or localities).

Local governments, civil society, and the private sector have emerged as significant counterparts in urban environmental management in developing countries and transition economies, and they are increasingly involved in project design and implementation. The private sector is providing services, through contractual and concession arrangements (figure 7-1).

The Role of Local Government

With decentralization, local governments have assumed a significant role in development projects. Because local governments are closest to project beneficiaries and often have more information on local concerns and more options available to address them, they are seen as the optimal local counterparts for implementing projects. However, government agencies (at the central or provincial level) and parastatals generally have the technical expertise—and generally the mandate—to manage urban environmental investments.

The role of local governments in Bank projects increased during the 1990s. In more than one-third of projects, the national authorities have delegated the task of implementing Bank projects to local governments (table 7-1). Local governments are also involved in project design in about one-fifth of projects, primarily in identifying subprojects. Local governments have a comparative advantage in being able to consult with project beneficiaries directly as well as through collaboration with civil society organizations. This is particularly valuable in projects that aim to provide basic environmental infrastructure and services, especially at the neighborhood level.

Figure 7-1. Counterparts Implementing World Bank-Funded Urban Environmental Projects

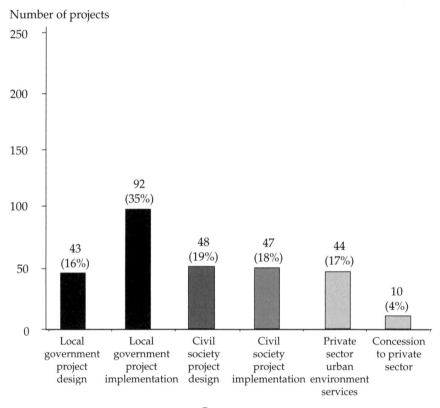

Note: Total exceeds 100 percent because multiple counterparts may be involved in the same projects.

The Role of Civil Society

The role of civil society has grown in importance in the development agenda. Civil society gives "voice" to local (as well as global) environmental concerns (Paul 1991); mobilizes community support for developmental projects; contributes to project design and implementation (by providing information on the social impacts of developmental projects or the maintenance of infrastructure and services, for example); and provides feedback on projects (by monitoring the provision of services).

Table 7-1. Involvement of Local Government, Civil Society, and the Private Sector in Designing and Implementing Urban Environmental Projects, by Goal

Urban environmental goal	Local government		Civil society		Private sector		Bank-wide
	Design	Implementation	Design	Implementation	Private sector participation	Concession	
Goal 1: Protect and enhance environmental health in urban areas	35	61	44	36	39	9	156
Goal 2: Protect water, soil, and air quality in urban areas from contamination and pollution	24	59	25	29	25	5	150
Goal 3: Minimize the urban impact on natural resources at regional and global scales	5	22	4	9	6	0	75
Goal 4: Prevent and mitigate urban impacts of natural disasters and climate change	1	5	1	1	0	0	22
Bank-wide	43	92	48	47	44	10	264

Note: Number of projects is greater than 264 because multiple counterparts may be involved in the same projects.

The increasing importance of civil society as a counterpart is reflected in Bank projects. Civil society is involved in project design, subproject identification, and project implementation in about one-fifth of active urban environmental projects. Bank projects build on the strengths of civil society, especially in the provision of basic environmental services to the urban poor (goals 1 and 2).

The Role of the Private Sector

The private sector has the potential to contribute to urban environmental management in many ways. (For a review of the interface between private sector development and environmental issues in Bank projects, see Abuyuan 2002.) It can, for example, play an important role in encouraging adoption of cleaner technology in industries, in providing urban environmental services, and in engaging in twinning arrangements for capacity building in public sector utilities. The private sector is participating in about one-fifth of the active projects under review. In nine projects concession agreements for the provision of services by the private sector are foreseen.

Involvement by Sector

Different Bank sectors involve local governments, civil society, and private sector in different capacities (table 7-2). Most sectors involve local governments in project design and implementation. Local government involvement is greatest in the Urban Development sector projects, where local governments are involved in more than half of all projects.

Civil society is involved mainly in Urban Development, Water and Sanitation, and Environment sector projects. Involvement is greatest in the Urban Development sector, particularly in project design. Civil society identifies needs for the provision of basic environmental services. Private sector participation is prevalent mainly in Water and Sanitation sector projects.

Table 7-2. Number of Urban Environmental Projects, by Sector and Counterpart

Sector	Local government		Civil society		Private sector		Total projects
	Design	Implementation	Design	Implementation	Private sector participation	Concession	
Water and Sanitation	11	27	15	11	29	6	85
Urban Development	24	31	21	17	5	2	60
Environment	2	14	5	11	3	0	45
Energy	2	7	0	1	5	2	23
Transport	0	6	0	1	1	0	23
Other	4	7	7	6	1	0	28
Bank-wide	43	92	48	47	44	10	264

Note: Number of projects is greater than 264 because multiple counterparts may be involved in the same projects.

8

Institutional Strengthening and Technical Assistance

Addressing urban environmental issues in developing countries warrants more than just a sector approach. Instruments need to be put in place to improve the ability to address technical and nontechnical issues, to provide environment-related and general technical assistance, and to support counterparts.

Appropriate regulatory frameworks are needed to facilitate better urban environmental management that cuts across sectors. Such frameworks are put in place through institutional strengthening in 45 percent of projects and through (concomitant) capacity building of the counterpart organizations in 65 percent of projects (figure 8-1).

Environment-related technical assistance provided by the Bank includes environmental action plans, environmental management plans, audits, monitoring and information systems, and public education on environmental issues. General technical assistance is related to policy formulation, preparation of strategies and sector plans, and specific project-related studies (one of the most frequently provided forms of technical assistance in the projects reviewed).

All sectors under review provide assistance for institutional strengthening and capacity building (table 8-1). The Environment sector provides the most environment-related technical assistance and environmental management in industries. Bank projects support counterparts in order to enhance their involvement in project design and implementation. Eleven percent of projects provide assistance for private sector development; five percent of projects support civil society involvement.

Figure 8-1. Projects That Strengthen Institutions or Provide Technical Assistance

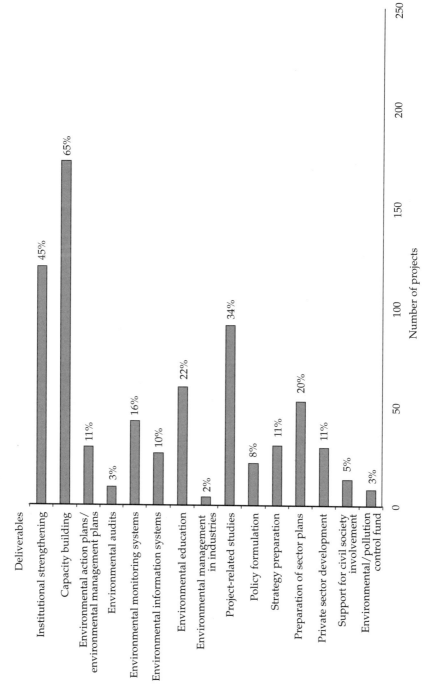

Table 8-1. Institutional Strengthening, Capacity Building, Technical Assistance, and Support to Counterparts, by Sector

Component	Water and Sanitation	Urban Development	Environment	Energy	Transport	Other	Total Bank-wide
Institutional strengthening	51	25	20	13	5	5	119
Capacity building	65	36	32	11	10	18	172
Environmental action and management plans	12	5	7	2	0	3	29
Environmental audits	3	1	5	0	0	0	9
Environmental monitoring systems	16	4	14	6	2	0	42
Environmental information systems	11	8	4	1	0	2	26
Environmental education	17	14	16	5	4	3	59
Environmental management in industries	1	0	3	0	0	0	4
Project-related studies	38	22	10	9	6	5	90
Policy formulation	8	5	6	2	0	0	21
Strategy preparation	6	8	4	0	12	0	30
Preparation of sector plans	19	18	7	1	4	3	52
Private sector development	13	6	3	6	0	1	29
Support for civil society involvement	6	3	2	0	0	2	13
Environmental/ pollution control fund	3	1	3	0	0	1	8
Total projects	85	60	45	23	23	28	264

Note: Number of projects is greater than 264 because projects support multiple activities.

9
Tracking the Quality of the Urban Environment Portfolio

The Bank tracks project implementation and periodically rates progress toward achieving development objectives by generating project supervision reports. On the basis of these reports, four measures of portfolio quality are periodically assessed: the percentage of projects at risk, the percentage of commitments at risk, realism (the ratio of actual problem projects to total actual and potential problem projects), and proactivity (the proportion of projects rated as problem projects 12 months earlier that have been upgraded, restructured, suspended, or partially or fully canceled).

The urban environment portfolio performs better than the overall Bank portfolio in terms of projects and commitments at risk. It has 3.5 percent fewer projects at risk and 7 percent fewer at-risk commitments than the portfolio of the Bank as a whole (figure 9-1). The percentage of urban environmental projects demonstrating realism (85 percent) is significantly higher than average for the Bank as a whole (62 percent).

The difference indicates that a higher proportion of urban environmental projects are encountering difficulties and are being rated as unsatisfactory on progress in implementation, on the achievement of development objectives, or both. The urban environment portfolio performed much worse than the Bank in terms of proactivity. Only 42 percent of projects in which problems had been identified the previous year had taken one of the recommended actions to respond to the problem (for the Bank as a whole the figure was 82 percent). Together these quality indicators suggest that urban environmental projects probably demand more intense supervision, better operational responses, and more effective adaptation to the realities on the ground in the implementation process to achieve their developmental objectives.

Figure 9-1. Quality of the Urban Environment and Overall Bank Portfolios, Third Quarter, Fiscal 2003

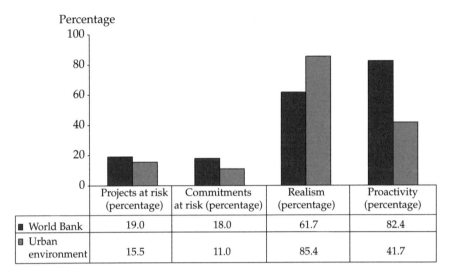

Percentage

	Projects at risk (percentage)	Commitments at risk (percentage)	Realism (percentage)	Proactivity (percentage)
▪ World Bank	19.0	18.0	61.7	82.4
▫ Urban environment	15.5	11.0	85.4	41.7

10
Using Monitoring Indicators to Measure Progress

The Bank has put increasing emphasis on improving the monitoring and evaluation of project implementation and outputs in recent years (Kolev and Nitti 2001; World Bank 2002c). Indicators are essential to monitor implementation progress and measure project outcomes.

In the Bank's Project Appraisal Documents, performance indicators are divided into output and impact indicators. Reference manuals have been prepared to help Bank Task Teams select and design performance indicators. For instance, Segnestam (1999) provides references on the way in which project outputs and impacts can be measured through Environmental Performance Indicators.

The review identified the kind of output and impact indicators used in the Bank's urban environmental projects. It also examined how expected project outputs and impacts relate to achievement of the Millennium Development Goals, where relevant.

Four kinds of environmental indicators are used:

- environmental health indicators (such as infant and child mortality rates)
- pollution reduction indicators (such as tons of pollution load removed)
- access to services indicators (such as increases in the percentage of the population with improved access to safe water supply)
- proxy operational indicators (such as the percentage of solid waste going to landfill or the length of sewer pipes replaced and rehabilitated)

Only about two-thirds of the projects reviewed use environmental indicators (figure 10-1). The small proportion probably reflects the difficulties and costs of creating baseline surveys identifying the state of the local environment before the investments take place. In addition, many of the projects reviewed were designed before monitoring and evaluation were emphasized as they are today. Environmental health indicators, which provide the best measure of the quality of life in urban areas, are used in only 5 percent of the projects.

Figure 10-1. Environmental Indicators Used in Urban
Environmental Projects

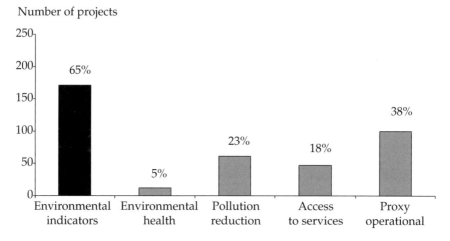

Using Indicators to Measure Progress toward Achieving Urban Environmental Goals

Different indicators are used to measure progress toward meeting different urban environmental goals (table 10-1). Access to services indicators are used in projects focusing on goals 1 and 2; pollution reduction indicators are used mainly in projects that address urban environmental goals 2 and 3. The use of proxy operational indicators is widespread and the use of environmental health indicators is limited.

Environmental health indicators—such as measuring the impact of providing water and sanitation services to the urban poor—are used chiefly by the Water and Sanitation sector (table 10-2). The main users of pollution reduction and abatement indicators are the Environment and Water and Sanitation sectors, which use them to measure pollution loads in rivers and streams, air pollution, and greenhouse gas emissions. A significant proportion of Water and Sanitation sector projects use access to services indicators, such as extension of water supply to unserved neighborhoods.

Using Indicators to Measure Progress toward Achieving the Millennium Development Goals

Bank projects that address urban environmental concerns are contributing to the achievement of many Millennium Development Goals and some of their key targets (figure 10-2). A major focus of Bank projects is integrating the

Table 10-1. Environmental Indicators Used to Measure Progress in Urban Environmental Projects, by Goal
(number of projects)

Urban environmental goal	Environ-mental health	Pollution reduction	Access to services	Proxy operational	Total projects
Goal 1: Protect and enhance environ-mental health in urban areas	10	27	43	66	156
Goal 2: Protect water, soil, and air quality in urban areas from contamination and pollution	7	46	36	61	150
Goal 3: Minimize the urban impact on natural resources at regional and global scales	1	34	6	28	75
Goal 4: Prevent and mitigate urban impacts of natural disasters and climate change	2	3	0	8	22
Bank-wide	12	61	47	100	264

Table 10-2. Urban Environmental Indicators Used, by Sector

Sector	Environmental health	Pollution reduction	Access to services	Proxy operational	Total projects
Water and Sanitation	9	22	34	39	85
Urban Development	1	7	7	27	60
Environment	1	20	4	11	45
Energy	0	8	0	8	23
Transport	0	2	0	7	23
Other	1	2	2	8	28
Bank-wide	12	61	47	100	264

principles of sustainable development policies and programs (target 9) in client countries' policies, a target that 82 percent of projects—and 100 percent of Energy sector projects—support (table 10-3). Achievement of this target can be measured through standard output indicators used in Bank projects. About half of all projects help achieve Millennium Development Goal targets 5, 6, 8, and 10. About one-third of all projects help achieve Millennium Development Goal target 11.

Millennium Development Goals (MDGs) Relevant to the Urban Environment

MDG 4: Reduce child mortality.

- Target 5 for 2015: Reduce the mortality rate among children under five by two-thirds.

MDG 5: Improve maternal health.

- Target 6 for 2015: Reduce the ratio of women dying in childbirth by three-quarters.

MDG 6: Combat HIV/AIDS, malaria, and other diseases.

- Target 8 for 2015: Halt and begin to reverse the spread of HIV/AIDS and the incidence of malaria and other major diseases.

MDG 7: Ensure environmental sustainability.

- Target 9: Integrate the principles of sustainable development into country policies and programs, and reverse the loss of environmental resources.
- Target 10: By 2015 reduce the proportion of people without access to safe drinking water by half.
- Target 11: By 2020 achieve significant improvement in the lives of at least 100 million slum dwellers.

Water and Sanitation, Urban Development, and "other" sectors invest in a high proportion of projects that support Millennium Development Goal targets 5, 6, 10, and 11. This arguably has a causal relationship with improvements in environmental health. But only a small fraction of projects in these sectors use environmental health indicators, leaving a crucial gap in measuring progress toward meeting the targets. A significant proportion of

Figure 10-2. Projects Contributing to Meeting Millennium Development Goal Targets

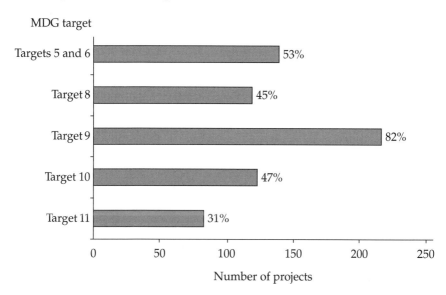

Note: Number of projects is greater than 264 because multiple MDG targets may be present in the same projects.

Table 10-3. Millennium Development Goal Targets of Urban Environmental Projects, by Sector

Sector	Targets 5 and 6	Target 8	Target 9	Target 10	Target 11	Total projects
Water and Sanitation	77	50	64	67	38	85
Urban Development	38	41	46	34	31	60
Environment	3	8	43	3	2	45
Energy	3	2	23	3	2	23
Transport	2	6	20	2	1	23
Other	16	12	20	14	9	28
Bank-wide	139	119	216	123	83	264

Note: Number of projects is greater than 264 because multiple MDG targets may be present in the same projects.

projects in all sectors except Energy contribute to achieving Millennium Development Goal target 8. There is a clear need to enhance the use of environmental indicators that could help measure progress toward achieving the Millennium Development Goal targets.

11
Strengths and Weaknesses of the Urban Environment Portfolio

The Bank's current commitment to improving urban environmental quality is strong. One out of five active operations includes activities or components that aim to improve the urban environment, and more than US$12 billion (12.6 percent of all active lending) is committed to the *expanded brown agenda.*

The fact that so many sectors are responsible for these operations shows that the urban environment is a cross-cutting field. Three-quarters of all Bank loans in this area are in the Water and Sanitation, Urban Development, and Energy sectors, confirming the importance of infrastructure investments to the urban environment. Such investments are critical not only to promote economic growth but also to generate more equitable access to basic services; improve quality of life, especially for the urban poor; and achieve environmental sustainability.

The portfolio review indicates that Bank operations are actively contributing to improving environmental health and protecting natural resources in and around urban areas. These issues are at the core of the *brown agenda* as defined at the beginning of the 1990s, when the majority of the operations reviewed were designed and approved.

Many of the operations reviewed cover several urban environmental challenges, some of which go beyond the direct competence of the sectors in charge, as some of the case studies show. Solid waste management projects are managed by the Water and Sanitation, Urban Development, and Environment sectors, revealing not only the importance of the issue but also the willingness of these sectors to integrate it with other project components, providing more synergies and ultimately better results on the ground. Sector responsibilities over specific aspects of urban environmental projects seem at times to overlap, given that operations targeting similar goals, such as extending water supply or providing sanitation, may be handled by different sectors in different regions.

Many operations are designed exclusively around single sector issues. This focus may allow projects to have greater impact on a particular issue, as they are often part of national efforts at sector reform that combine invest-

STRENGTHS AND WEAKNESSES OF THE URBAN ENVIRONMENT PORTFOLIO   57

ments with enforcement of new policies. Such operations may be forgoing the opportunity to provide holistic coverage of environmental priorities, however.

The majority of the projects reviewed appear to be contributing to the achievement of the Millennium Development Goals. These projects are reducing infant and child mortality, reducing the incidence of major diseases, integrating sustainable development into national policies and programs, reducing the percentage of people without access to safe drinking water, and improving the lives of slum dwellers.

In addition to the physical investments, these operations also provide the opportunity to support important processes for defining, approving, and implementing sector reforms; putting in place or reinforcing sector institutions and agencies; and improving the participation of local governments, civil society, and the private sector in providing urban environmental services. If these improvements and innovations are maintained and applied more broadly by the Bank's borrowers, they may bring significant benefits that extend well beyond the scope of the projects themselves.

In all of the Bank's regions and nearly all of its client countries, the Bank is supporting research and the dissemination of its findings, and opportunities for capacity building and learning, either independently or through partnerships. All of these activities draw from the lending operations, and the project counterparts generally benefit from them.

The portfolio review has also highlighted some areas of concern:

- Investments in the cities of South Asia seem to fall short of needs. Although South Asian cities make up 20 percent of the world's urban population, they account for just 9 percent of the Bank's urban environmental lending. On a per urban capita basis, Bank investment in the region is less than one-third the average figure.
- Smaller cities are the beneficiaries of a disproportionate share of Bank projects. Although about half of the urban population of the Bank's client countries live in cities with less than 1 million inhabitants, more than two-thirds of the Bank's urban projects are located in such cities. This may mean that the urban environmental challenges of larger agglomerations, especially megacities, may not be addressed as fully as they could be.
- Indoor air quality and urban air pollution are not adequately addressed in the urban environment portfolio: the Bank supports only 4 projects on improving indoor air quality, 18 providing vehicular or industrial emissions control, and 8 promoting the use of cleaner fuels for vehicles and more efficient public transportation systems. Current levels of morbidity and mortality caused by poor indoor and urban air quality suggest that the Bank's contribution may be too modest, particularly given

the importance of air quality issues in the Bank's own corporate strategies and analytical work.

• Pollution from small and medium-size enterprises and from the semi-industrial activities of the informal sector are not addressed by the Bank's urban environment portfolio. Studies on the sources of urban pollution across the developing world confirm that small and medium-size enterprises and the informal sector are important sources of pollution that affect natural resources, the environmental health of the resident population, and their own labor forces. The environmental management systems and regulatory frameworks that the Bank helps sector institutions set in place are rarely applied to such small-scale operators.

12
Recommendations for Future Work

This review did not cover the next generation of urban environmental projects—those currently being designed or under preparation. The review of the pipeline might reveal that some of the concerns raised are being addressed by the next generation of investments.

The review did not cover the Bank's knowledge services, such as analytical and advisory work, technical assistance, and capacity building. In recent years, the Bank has financed a significant volume of knowledge services to its clients, and some of the concerns highlighted may have been at least partially addressed.

Several recommendations can be made that reflect the new directions development assistance is taking and the need to pursue a broader, *expanded brown agenda*:

- The linkages among environment, poverty, and health in urban areas need to be better mainstreamed in the Bank's work. The *expanded brown agenda* needs to be better recognized and introduced in Country Assistance Strategy and Poverty Reduction Strategy discussions, when the Bank and client governments negotiate priority areas for Bank intervention and support. Country environmental analyses and sector environmental analyses could be the appropriate tools for this mainstreaming to take place.
- The next generation of urban environmental projects will have to include a better set of environmental indicators, in order to establish the positive impacts that operations are having on the quality of life, the livability of cities, and the protection of the regional and global commons. To demonstrate the contribution of its lending operations to the achievement of the Millennium Development Goals, the Bank has undertaken a major effort to provide projects with more detailed impact indicators. These indicators may eventually be "retrofitted" to several active operations, including some in the urban environment portfolio.
- As the *expanded brown agenda* becomes more widely recognized, Bank operations should more forcefully address mitigation of and adaptation to cli-

mate change. Increasing climate variability, the growing number and intensity of natural disasters due to climate change, and the increase in sea level are becoming bigger parts of the daily challenges facing cities in the developing world, 70 percent of which are located on coasts. These new challenges threaten quality of life, productivity and competitiveness, and in some cases the very ability of these cities to survive.

• Before such new areas can be mainstreamed as part of lending operations, the Bank's research and analytical work must embrace the *expanded brown agenda* more fully. It must devote resources to exploring some emerging new issues including, for instance, the opportunities for urban regeneration represented by brownfields reclamation. This has yielded interesting results in OECD countries, but remains largely unexplored in the developing world, despite obvious opportunities in regions such as Latin America and the Caribbean and South and East Asia, and some successful operations.

For progress to be made in any of these areas, collaboration between the Infrastructure and Environment units at both the central and regional levels needs to move beyond simple compliance with the Bank's environmental safeguards policies. Active collaboration is needed to promote more and better infrastructure investments to improve the urban environment in a sustainable manner.

More collaboration is also needed among the four sectors that are part of the Bank's Infrastructure Vice Presidency (Water and Sanitation, Urban Development, Energy, and Transport), so that synergies can be captured at the outset of project design. In the future, for example, improvement of storm-water drainage and solid waste collection, or of disaster preparedness and slum upgrading, should be pursued as interrelated development objectives.

To facilitate further integration of the urban environmental challenges, multidisciplinary Bank teams working in close collaboration with local counterparts could generate Rapid Urban Environmental Profiles. This tool provides a quick review of the major environmental issues a city faces, highlights the city's priorities, and helps in understanding the complex links among the various environmental challenges.

During the 1990s, the pursuit of a holistic approach to urban environmental management was promoted through strategic planning. Many multilateral and bilateral development agencies, as well as many nongovernmental organizations engaged in comprehensive strategic planning exercises, often along the lines of the Local Agenda 21 principles. The Bank endorsed this approach, but it was not extensively applied in the Bank's operational work, because of the time and financial resources required to carry out comprehensive urban environmental strategies. The need to conduct stakeholder consultations was difficult to integrate into the normal project preparation cycle. Urban environmental strategies carried out independently often caused local frustration, as the participatory definition of the priorities and action plans was not followed by investments.

The preparation of a city-specific Rapid Urban Environmental Profile would not be a complex, costly, and cumbersome exercise but rather an overview of the environmental challenges a city is facing. It would constitute the basis for a common understanding of priorities, which would then be addressed in the design of parallel interrelated sector loans or of a single operation. Country team support for a common effort that would pool specialists—generally confined to work programs determined by their sector affiliations—would be essential for its implementation.

This recommendation was approved by the joint meeting of the Water and Sanitation, Urban Development, and Environment Sector Boards that met to discuss the preliminary findings of the urban environment portfolio review in December 2002.

Given the importance of the Infrastructure sectors in improving the urban environment, it is recommended that the Rapid Urban Environmental Profiles be prepared as part of, or in conjunction with, the infrastructure assessments being promoted by the Infrastructure Vice-Presidency.

II
Case Studies

Overview of Case Studies

Twelve case studies were developed to illustrate the multisector nature of the urban environment portfolio and the integrated approach needed to address urban environmental issues (see table). The cases represent typical project deliverables found in the Bank's urban environmental work in the five main sectors (Urban Development, Environment, Water and Sanitation, Energy, and Transport) but also innovative ones. The case studies were drafted using public information for the descriptive data, the authors' subjective statements on the urban environmental aspects of the projects, and the Bank supervising Task Team Leaders' judgments on implementation progress.

Case Studies of Projects with Urban Environmental Goals

Project	Project city	Urban environmental goal	Urban environmental issues addressed
Water and Sanitation			
China: Liaoning Environment	Anshan, Dalian, Fushun, Benxi, Jinzhou	1, 2, 3	Wastewater management, clean technology
India: Bombay Sewage Disposal	Mumbai	1, 2	Sewage disposal, sanitation in slums
Colombia: Cartagena Water Supply, Sewerage, and Environmental Management	Cartagena	1, 2	Water supply and sewerage
Urban Development			
Guinea: Third Urban Development	Conakry	1, 2	Urban services, including solid waste management
RB de Venezuela: Caracas Slum Upgrading	Caracas	1	Urban upgrading
Nicaragua: Natural Disaster Vulnerability Reduction	Secondary cities	4	Disaster management

(*Continued on the following page.*)

Case Studies of Projects with Urban Environmental Goals

(continued)

Project	Project city	Urban environmental goal	Urban environmental issues addressed
Environment			
Latvia: Municipal Solid Waste Management	Riga	3	Solid waste management, groundwater pollution, greenhouse gas reduction
Algeria: Industrial Pollution Control	Annaba	2, 3	Industrial pollution
Kenya, Tanzania, Uganda: Lake Victoria Environmental Management	Kampala, Mwanza, Kisumu	2	Water resources and coastal zone management
Energy			
Poland: Krakow Energy Efficiency	Krakow, Skawina	3	District heating, energy efficiency
Mongolia: Improved Household Stoves in Urban Centers	Ulaanbaatar	1, 2, 3	Indoor and ambient air pollution, energy efficiency
Transport			
China: Guangzhou City Center Transport	Guangzhou	2	Air quality management

Goal 1: Protect and enhance environmental health in urban areas.
Goal 2: Protect the water, soil, and air quality in urban areas from contamination and pollution.
Goal 3: Minimize the urban impact on natural resources at the regional and global scales.
Goal 4: Prevent and mitigate the urban impacts of natural disasters and climate change.

China:
Liaoning Environment Project

Project Data

Project title: Liaoning Environment Project (P003598)
Sector: Water and Sanitation
Region: East Asia and Pacific
Country: China
Cities and size of cities: Anshan, 2.42 million; Benxi, 1.18 million; Dalian, 3.32 million; Fushun, 1.43 million; Jinzhou, 1.3 million
Sector codes: Sewerage (67 percent), district heating and energy efficiency services (25 percent), solid waste management (6 percent), other social services (2 percent)
Theme codes: Water resources management (primary), environmental policies and institutions (primary), pollution management and environmental health (primary), climate change (secondary)
Amount of loan and total project value: US$110 million, US$350.8 million
Fiscal year of approval: 1994
Scheduled closing date: December 31, 2003
Task Team Leader: Rajagopal S. Iyer, Lead Management Specialist, East Asia and Pacific Urban Development Sector Unit

Project Profile

Development objectives: This project aims to protect the main water resources in Liaoning Province, including the Hun-Taizi river basin, to allow sustained economic and safe use for drinking, industrial, and agricultural purposes; to strengthen pricing policies and institutional arrangements for environment protection, water pollution control, and wastewater and municipal solid waste management; and to institute measures to control air pollution and manage cultural heritage assets.

Benefits and target population: The project is expected to significantly mitigate environmental degradation and yield both economic and social benefits for Liaoning Province, an area of serious and concentrated water and air pollution, largely of industrial origin. Project components are designed to both reduce pollution and improve operational efficiency through technological upgrading and waste minimization and reuse. Control of water pollution at industrial sites is expected to reduce costs for water treatment and urban water supply. Health benefits are expected to accrue from the reduction of waterborne diseases, while reduced emissions of toxic gases into the atmosphere are expected to decrease respiratory ailments and cancer and reduce corrosive damage to buildings. The project is also expected to improve operational efficiency in solid waste collection and disposal. The innovative heritage conservation components protect cultural assets from further damage and display and restore unique world-class cultural property for sustained public use. Finally, the project hopes to contribute to the sustainability of environmental management in the province by demonstrating cost-effective pollution control measures, strengthening local capabilities in the monitoring and enforcement of environmental regulations, corporatizing the sewerage utilities, and establishing a sound cost recovery policy for pollution abatement services.

Project description (components): The project provides physical works and technical assistance for institutional development in water supply, wastewater treatment, air pollution control, waste management, water conservation and process improvements, and environmental rehabilitation and reconstruction. Project components include the following:

- *Wastewater management in Anshan and Fushun*: Construction of sewers, pump stations, wastewater treatment, and effluent reuse facilities
- *Wastewater and air quality management in Benxi*: Construction of sewers, pump stations, and primary wastewater treatment facilities; introduction of an air quality management program, including equipment and facilities to reduce emissions from two blast furnaces and three coke ovens and increase their energy efficiency; and provision of district heating to serve some 20,000 households over an area of some 300 hectares
- *Wastewater, municipal solid waste, and water conservation management investments in Dalian*: Construction of sewers, construction of a new secondary wastewater treatment plant and the upgrading of the existing plant, and construction of effluent reuse facilities; introduction of a pilot water conservation and clean technology program; and investments in solid waste management, including modernization of the municipal collection, transfer and transportation systems, upgrading of the existing disposal facility to sanitary landfill standards, and providing for future landfill gas utilization

- *Water supply system enhancement and protection in Jinzhou*: Protection of groundwater and enhancement of trunk supply, upgrading of the treatment plant and strengthening of the distribution system, and reduction in pollution and conservation of water by the Jincheng Paper Mill
- *Environmental rehabilitation and reconstruction*: Recording, rehabilitation, conservation, protection, restoration, and display of prioritized cultural heritage assets of world significance, including the Liaoning Great Wall at Jiumenkou, archeological sites at Niuheliang and Jieshi Gong, and the Shenyang Provincial Museum
- *Liaoning Environment Fund*: Creation of a fund for the provision of short-term finance for focused high-impact investments in in-plant clean technology processes that support the core investments in air and wastewater management
- *Institutional strengthening*: Technical assistance and training for supporting and strengthening environmental, financial and utility management and performance monitoring, training, feasibility studies, and future project preparation

Strategic choices: Liaoning Province, in northeastern China, has a population of about 36 million, including some 25 million urban residents. The province has a strong urban industrial base. Its basic food supply comes from farming in several large river basins. The most important of these are the twin basins of the Hun and Taizi rivers, which represent 20 percent of the province's land area, produce about 40 percent of its agricultural and 60 percent of its industrial output, and contain about 13 million people. Water supply for industrial, domestic, and agricultural purposes depends heavily on flows from the two rivers. Rapid industrial development combined with inappropriate wastewater management has polluted both surface water and groundwater resources with organic matter, toxic chemicals, oils, and heavy metals, seriously affecting drinking, industrial, and agricultural water quality. There is an urgent need to raise the quality of the water in the two rivers to a standard that is environmentally safe, economically usable, and sustainable. The Liaoning provincial government has begun to curb the discharge of heavy metals and toxic chemicals from the major polluting industries, with some success. The remaining pollution abatement has to be done at the city level, something that most cities are still not equipped to do.

Strategies for the effective utilization of the Hun-Taizi water resources were developed by a river basin management study, which identified and ranked a set of investments for water resource development and water pollution abatement in specific cities. The study also highlighted deficiencies in institutional arrangements for water resource management, identified inadequate urban environmental services, and stressed the need for focused water and wastewater investments. A Bank-financed project—the Liaoning Urban Infrastructure Project, approved in 1990 and implemented by the Liaoning Urban Construction and Renewal Project Office (LUCRPO)—supports water supply in the basin cities of Shenyang, Fuxin, and Yingkou and measures that will strengthen industrial pollution control. Implementation of that project has been rated satisfactory. This project complements earlier projects and finances a priority set of investments focusing on environmental management and pollution abatement.

Institutional arrangements for management and implementation differ. In addition to LUCRPO, a provincial project office set up by the Liaoning Construction Commission under the Liaoning Urban Infrastructure Project, four municipal-level project offices have been established, one each for the water components in the three project cities and one for urban transport in Shenyang. LUCRPO is responsible for managing project preparation, coordinating implementation, and monitoring execution.

LUCRPO is responsible for overall project coordination and macro-level project management and monitoring; project-wide quality assurance; progress reporting to the Liaoning provincial government and the Bank, including reporting on cost management, project impact, and environmental improvement assessment; interagency coordination and procurement support; and facilitation of sector training. Municipal-level project offices have been established in Anshan, Benxi, Dalian, Fushun, Jinxi, and Jinzhou. The project components for wastewater, air, solid waste, water supply, heating, and process improvements in Anshan, Benxi, Dalian, and Jinzhou are being carried out by specific companies. The activities under the environmental rehabilitation component are being carried out by the Liaoning provincial government, the Jinxi municipal government, and the Jimi municipal government. The project component on environmental impact investments in industrial enterprises is being carried out by the Liaoning Environment Fund, with the Liaoning Environmental Protection Bureau acting as the on-lending agency. The technical assistance and training component is being implemented by LUCRPO, the Liaoning Finance Bureau, and the Liaoning Environmental Protection Bureau.

Institutional strengthening and technical assistance activities: The institutional development and policy strengthening components are expected to enhance policies and operational experience in environmental protection, wastewater reduction, water pollution control, and heritage asset management. These initiatives include the following:

- establishing appropriate pricing policies for management of wastewater, solid waste, and cultural heritage assets

- improving measures for water pollution monitoring, enforcing water pollution regulations, and establishing appropriate water pollution charges
- creating an environment fund to support industrial wastewater treatment facilities, process modernization, and clean technology
- training staff engaged in financial management, water pollution control, and wastewater and municipal solid waste management
- providing technical assistance for studies and future project preparation, including measures to alleviate air pollution, and environmental infrastructure master planning
- formulating and preparing potential future investment projects

Urban Environmental Aspects

The project targets urban environmental goals 1 (protect and enhance environmental health in urban areas); 2 (protect water, soil, and air quality in urban areas from contamination and pollution); and 3 (minimize the urban impact on natural resources at the regional and global scales). The project builds on prior analytical work that identified interrelated issues of infrastructure and service provision and the environmental management that affect both quality of life and archaeological and cultural heritage, as well as the appropriate institutional arrangements. The project takes a holistic approach to wastewater, solid waste, and air quality management, with a focus on local and global issues through cross-sectoral interventions. It includes components that complement earlier Bank projects on water conservation and clean technology, and it introduces an innovative cultural heritage component within an urban environmental context.

The project uses pollution reduction indicators, including the reduction in sodium dioxide and total suspended particles to improve air quality in Benxi and the percentage reduction in nightsoil. It also uses proxy operational indicators, such as enhancement of drinking water quality to achieve Class HI standard, identification and control of sources of pollution (percent of system connections in each city), and landfill usage to improve municipal solid waste and nightsoil management. The project lacks environmental health indicators to measure these benefits, however.

Ongoing Implementation

The project is rated satisfactory on development objectives. It is rated satisfactory on all specific rating indices except financial performance and monitoring indicators, where performance has been unsatisfactory. There are no pending issues. The physical works have been substantially completed, and water resources along the Hun-Taizi river basin have improved. Project agencies are now more focused on institutional reform and financial sustainability issues, including tariff levels and collection. Air pollution measures have been instituted, and loan savings are being used to make further improvements to air quality in Benxi. The cultural heritage component has been substantially completed. Land acquisition and resettlement work under the project have been completed. In general, project components are contributing to the improvement of the urban environment.

India: Bombay Sewage Disposal Project

Project Data

Project title: Bombay Sewage Disposal Project (P010480)
Sector: Water and Sanitation
Region: South Asia
Country: India
City and size of city: Mumbai (Bombay), 17.01 million
Sector codes: Sewerage (90 percent), sanitation (10 percent)
Theme codes: Municipal governance and institutions (primary), pollution management and environmental health (primary), access to urban services for the poor (primary)
Amount of loan and total project value: US$192 million, US$295.6 million
Fiscal year of approval: 1996
Scheduled closing date: December 31, 2003
Task Team Leader: Shyamal Sarkar, Senior Sanitary Engineer, South Asia Energy and Infrastructure Unit

Project Profile

Development objectives: This project aims to strengthen the capacity of the Water Supply and Sewerage Department of the Municipal Corporation of Greater Bombay (MCGB) in all aspects of managing the provision of sewerage services; to sustain the financial viability of the provision of water supply and sewerage services in Greater Mumbai through direct charges to beneficiaries at appropriate levels; and to improve health and environmental conditions in Greater Mumbai, including conditions faced by slum dwellers.

Benefits and target population: The project is expected to help dispose of more than 60 percent of sewage from the Greater Mumbai area, yielding substantial health and environmental benefits. Together with the three Bombay Water Supply and Sewerage Projects (BWSSP I, II, and III), the project is expected to connect 45 percent of the population of Greater Mumbai to a waterborne sewerage system capable of conveying domestic and industrial wastes to facilities for partial treatment and disposal. Pavement dwellers and slum residents are not served by the system. Some of their needs will be addressed by the slum sanitation schemes included in the project.

The slum sanitation component is expected to alleviate the harsh living conditions of some 1 million slum dwellers—mainly people occupying municipally owned lands—by improving sanitation facilities, primarily for safe disposal of excreta. The direct benefits of the project will come from removing domestic sewage and industrial wastes from the inner city's natural water courses, surface water drains, shoreline, and beaches. These efforts will improve the living conditions of the urban population living near the city's many open sewers, reduce health risks, and improve the city's aesthetic environment.

Project description (components): The project finances the construction or rehabilitation of sewerage-related infrastructure. Specific components include the following:

- construction of two submarine tunnel outfall sewers in Worli and Bandra to convey partially treated sewage effluent to the Arabian Sea
- construction of a pumping station in Bandra
- construction of two aerated sewage treatment lagoons at Ghatkopar and Bhandup
- construction of facilities to prevent siltation in the influent tunnel at Ghatkopar
- rehabilitation of the Ghatkopar tunnel
- improvement of the structural stability of five sewage pumping stations
- improvement of conveyance systems
- introduction of slum sanitation schemes

The project also includes technical and social services to help implement the physical works, upgrade the operational and maintenance capabilities of MCGB with respect to Mumbai's sewerage system, and plan and design a second-stage program to improve health and environmental conditions.

Strategic choices: Mumbai is India's largest city and the country's preeminent center of trade, commerce, and finance. It accounts for 30 percent of the value of India's industrial production and an estimated 10 percent of India's industrial employment. Annual average population growth of 4.3 percent between 1981 and 1991 in the city was significantly higher than the 3.1 percent average for India's urban areas, and the provision of basic infrastructure did not keep pace with such growth. Over the past 50 years, higher priority was accorded to water supply than to sanitary sewerage. Together with financial resource constraints, this emphasis led to a situation in which only a very small area of the city was served by a piped sewerage system. The rest of the urban area discharged wastewater indiscriminately into surface water streams, gullies, and open storm-water drains.

Attempts to reverse this situation were undertaken through the Bank-assisted BWSSP I, II, and III projects. BWSSP I and II ran into cost overruns and time delays; BWSSP III focused primarily on water supply. This project is a logical follow-up to the first and second projects. It includes most of the first stage of development of facilities to partially treat and dispose of sewage collected and conveyed to proposed treatment and disposal sites by facilities constructed under the earlier projects. Without this project, it is conceivable that the benefits of the earlier projects would never be fully realized.

Under this project, some partially treated sewage from two drainage areas is discharged into the Arabian Sea at a distance of three kilometers from the shoreline. Sewage from two other drainage areas is discharged into tidal creeks after receiving the equivalent of primary treatment. Although not ideal, this solution is considered a significant improvement over the previous situation, in which sewage was discharged on the shoreline and into surface water drains and channels in heavily populated urban areas. Under the project, a time-bound program is to be established, leading to a second-stage program of sewage treatment and disposal facilities that will upgrade the quality of receiving waters.

Institutional and implementation arrangements (counterparts): The project is implemented by MCGB's Water Supply and Sewerage Department, with the assistance of foreign and local consultants. International consultants supervise the major components of the project, including construction of the Worli and Bandra outfalls, the Bandra pumping station, and the facilities to control siltation in the Ghatkopar Influent Tunnel. Local consultants supervise construction of the Ghatkopar and Bhandup lagoons, the slum sanitation component, structural improvements in five pumping stations, and improvements to the conveyance system.

MCGB, the largest municipal corporation in India, was established under the Bombay Municipal Corporation Act of 1888. The implementing agency for the project, the Water Supply and Sewerage Department of MCGB, was established in 1973. It is responsible for the planning, development, and operation and maintenance of water supply and sewerage services in Greater Mumbai. The Municipal Commissioner, MCGB's principal officer, maintains overall responsibility for the Water Supply and Sewerage Department.

Project management of BWSSP II and III was not satisfactory, particularly with regard to their sewerage components. In 1991, following the Bank's request for the appointment of a more experienced and senior manager to take control of these projects, management responsibility was assigned to the Additional Municipal Commissioner, a senior civil servant from the Indian Administrative Service. This arrangement continues and has resulted in marked improvement in the overall management of the Water Supply and Sewerage Department. For this project MCGB maintains a project management unit in the Water Supply and Sewerage Department. Specialists manage the slum sanitation schemes, procurement processes, environmental mitigation, and monitoring plans.

Institutional strengthening and technical assistance activities: Technical assistance includes project support; studies, site investigations, and engineering for second-stage works; and complementary studies. Consultants supervise construction; help upgrade the Water Supply and Sewerage Department's operation and maintenance practices in the sewerage system; help conduct required surveys, map the conveyance system, and formulate a program of conveyance system improvements and preventive maintenance; and assist, together with NGOs, in improving sanitary conditions in Mumbai's slums.

The project supports planning for higher levels of treatment and improved disposal methods in sewage treatment and disposal facilities for second-stage works. This support includes conducting feasibility studies for second-stage sewage treatment and disposal facilities in six drainage areas and completing detailed engineering designs for sewage treatment and disposal facilities in the six drainage areas. The project also supports several complementary technical studies for additional improvements to the sewerage system. Training programs initiated under BWSSP II and III are to be continued during implementation of this project. The project also provides training to upgrade the operation and maintenance levels of the entire sewerage system for Mumbai, and specific training of MCGB personnel to improve job skills and operation and management efficiency.

Urban Environmental Aspects

The project targets urban environmental goals 1 (protect and enhance environmental health in urban areas) and 2 (protect water, soil, and air quality in urban areas from contamination and pollution). The entire loan (US$192 million) is allocated to addressing urban environmental issues.

The project integrates the urban environmental issues of infrastructure and service provision for sewage collection, treatment, and disposal. It aims to build viability in the provision of water supply and sewerage services in Greater Mumbai through direct charges to beneficiaries, adding to its long-term economic and environmental sustainability. By closing down open sewers and providing services to slum dwellers, the project improves environmental health and reduces potential loss of life.

The project uses two access to service indicators: the number of sewerage connections and the number of latrine seats constructed. As an environmental health indicator, the project is measuring the number of reported cases of waterborne diseases. The project is also establishing and measuring health indicators in the slums in which the sanitation schemes are being implemented.

Ongoing Implementation

The project is substantially completed, except for the sanitation schemes in slums. The submarine tunnel outfalls at Worli and Bandra and the aerated lagoons at Bhandup and Ghatkopar have been completed and commissioned. All sewerage improvements have also been completed. No-dig technology was used extensively to install sewers in difficult stretches and to rehabilitate old sewers. The slum sanitation program implementation, which started late, is ongoing. Some 212 schemes were expected to have been completed by the end of June 2003. Another 100 ongoing schemes were expected to have been completed by the end of 2003.

Changes were made to the conveyance of sewage to the Ghatkopar lagoons based on a detailed study undertaken during implementation. Plans to construct facilities to prevent siltation in the influent tunnel at Ghatkopar and to rehabilitate the existing Ghatkopar tunnel were dropped. Instead, a new tunnel was constructed.

Major difficulties were encountered in implementing the demand-led participatory slum sanitation schemes, in which the community was to share the cost of construction and then take over operation and maintenance responsibilities. These difficulties have been partially overcome, through a process of learning-by-doing capacity building for stakeholders. A flexible approach to stepping up implementation has been adopted, and partnerships have been built between the community, local government bodies, and civil society.

Key lessons learned from the implementation include the following:

• Design and supervision of complex engineering works and the associated environmental management can be delegated to consultants.
• The right framework for facilitating partnerships among stakeholders is better developed through initial investment than by learning by doing.

- Local communities need to develop a sense of ownership and to be involved in project design if community-based programs are to be sustainable.
- Providing sanitation services to slums is not effective without providing water and electricity.
- Initial assessment and clear identification of baseline data and indicators and the use of appropriate monitoring and evaluation are very important to support the implementation process and evaluate the impact of the investments on the ground.

Colombia: Cartagena Water Supply, Sewerage, and Environmental Management Project

Project Data

Project title: Cartagena Water Supply, Sewerage, and Environmental Management Project (P044140)
Sector: Water and Sanitation
Region: Latin America and the Caribbean
Country: Colombia
City and size of city: Cartagena, 900,000
Sector codes: Water supply (11 percent), sanitation (85 percent), subnational government administration (4 percent)
Theme codes: Access to urban services for the poor (primary), pollution management and environmental health (primary), other financial and private sector development (secondary)
Amount of loan and total project value: US$85 million, US$117.2 million
Year of approval: 1999
Scheduled closing date: December 31, 2004
Task Team Leader: Menahem Libhaber, Lead Sanitary Engineer, Latin America and the Caribbean Water and Sanitation Cluster

Project Profile

Development objectives: This project aims to improve the water and sewerage services of Cartagena and the sanitary conditions of the city's poorest population by expanding water and sewerage coverage, particularly in the city's poor neighborhoods; to facilitate the environmental cleanup of water bodies surrounding the city (Cartagena Bay, the Caribbean beaches, and Cienaga de la Virgen Lake) by providing adequate collection, treatment, and disposal of the entire flow of the city's wastewater; and to improve the sustainability of water and sewerage services in Cartagena by leveraging Bank support to shore up the private sector participation model pioneered by ACUACAR (Aguas de Cartagena, the water and sewerage company of Cartagena) against political interference.

Benefits and target population: The project is expected to bring significant public health benefits in terms of sanitation services, especially in the city's poor and marginal areas. It will also improve overall standards of living in the city, especially in poor neighborhoods around the Cienaga Lake, and reduce urban pollution throughout the city. The project will enhance socioeconomic development in the region, which depends on tourism, and bring indirect benefits to the tourism industry by reducing environmental pollution and public health risks.

About 80,000 people in the city's poorest neighborhoods (especially in the San Jose de Los Campanos, El Pozón, Villa Estrella, La Boquilla, Paseo Bolivar, Zona Suroccidental, and Zona Suroriental sub-basins, which currently discharge their sewage to the Cienaga) will directly benefit from project investments that increase sewerage and water supply coverage. In Cartagena as a whole, about 750,000 inhabitants will benefit from improvements in the reliability of the water supply service and especially from the environmental improvements that wastewater collection, treatment, and safe disposal systems will bring to the Caribbean beaches, Cienaga Lake, Cartagena Bay, and other water courses that cross the city. The 700,000 tourists who visit Cartagena per year will benefit from the environmental improvements brought about by the project. While tourism and associated economic growth depend on a variety of factors beyond the direct control of this project, the promotion of Cartagena's tourism industry and its impact on the city's economic growth are major indirect benefits.

Project description (components): The project includes the following components:

- expansion of the water supply system to cover water production systems, increasing water coverage; replacement of the primary distribution mains, including mitigation of the water treatment sludge environmental impact; and preparation of a plan for reducing unaccounted-for-water
- expansion of the sewerage system in the Cienaga basin to enhance the conveyance capacity of sewage collectors that currently drain into the basin, expansion of secondary sewerage within this part of the city, and construction of new pressure lines, pumping stations, and gravity collectors in residential areas
- construction of the main wastewater conveyance system, using reinforced concrete pressure pipes
- construction of wastewater treatment installations
- construction of a submarine out-fall
- control of industrial wastewater discharge
- other measures to mitigate the environmental and social impacts of the project

Strategic choices: The project addresses three significant sector priorities: expanding insufficient water and sewerage coverage, giving greater emphasis to the treatment and adequate disposal of wastewater to reduce water pollution, and supporting private sector participation arrangements to improve the financial and operational efficiency of water and sanitation services. Some of the major institutional changes (primarily creation of ACUACAR as a mixed-capital utility) were supported under a previous loan, the Water Supply and Sewerage Sector Project (Loan 2961-CO). The related physical investments were deferred to this project.

The components of this project have been strategically selected to complement investments being implemented with funding from the District of Cartagena, ACUACAR, and the Inter-American Development Bank (IDB) in areas that discharge into Cartagena Bay, in the hotel area of Bocagrande, and in the southwestern part of the city. The project aims to complete the city sewage collection program and provide treatment and disposal for all wastewater generated throughout the city. The project is thus key to capturing the full health and environmental benefits of investments made by all parties.

Institutional and implementation arrangements (counterparts): The borrower for the project is the District of Cartagena. The project is being implemented by a project implementation unit within ACUACAR. ACUACAR is a well-managed public-private water and sewerage service company with private management. Its operational performance meets the highest international standards. The project implementation unit within ACUACAR is in charge of the entire investment program for all projects financed by ACUACAR, the District of Cartagena, and IDB. The project implementation unit worked efficiently with the Bank under the previous loan and during project preparation, and it is familiar with the Bank's procurement guidelines as well as project preparation and implementation procedures. It enjoys the support of the technical department of ACUACAR, which has a highly qualified staff.

The project implementation unit also has access to the technology and support of the AGBAR group (Aguas de Barcelona—the water and sewerage company of Barcelona). In addition, consulting firms have helped the unit design and supervise highly specialized works. Panels of experts, who served as the project steering committee, have also advised the unit. The project implementation unit is in charge of designing and supervising routine works. Its staff had access to substantive training on various aspects of project management.

Institutional strengthening and technical assistance activities: The project supports several institutional strengthening and technical assistance activities, including project management, technical assistance, studies, and design and supervision of works. These activities include project management; design and supervision of the water supply systems works; design and supervision of the sewerage systems works; design of the main wastewater conveyance system, treatment installations, and submarine outfall; supervision of the main conveyance system works; and supervision of the treatment installation and submarine outfall works. Specific activities supported under project management include the financing of consultants hired by the project implementation unit; assistance in completing detailed engineering designs; preparation of bidding documents for the purchase of equipment and the execution of works; preparation of letters of invitation and corresponding packages for hiring consultants and carrying out required procurement processes; and assistance in supervising all works and carrying out the financial management activities of the project.

Urban Environmental Aspects

The project targets urban environmental goals 1 (protect and enhance environmental health in urban areas) and 2 (protect water, soil, and air quality in urban areas from contamination and pollution). The entire loan (US$85 million) is allocated to addressing urban environmental issues.

The project integrates different urban environmental concerns, such as provision of water supply in low-income areas, water conservation through reduction of unaccounted-for water, construction of sewerage network and wastewater conveyance systems, treatment of wastewater, and environmental cleanup of water bodies in an urban space.

The project addresses environmental health and poverty issues of the low-income population (arguably leading to reductions in health expenditure and increases in household income). The environmental health benefits of the project cannot be measured, however, because the project does not include health indicators. The project also aims to improve the economy of the city by providing indirect benefits to the tourism industry. In doing so, it promotes public-private partnership in ACUACAR and involves civil society in project design.

The project uses pollution reduction indicators (such as the level of pathogenic coliform contamination along the beaches of Cartagena, the bay, and Cienaga Lake) and access to services indicators (such as coverage of water supply and sewerage network).

Ongoing Implementation

Project implementation progress is satisfactory. Implementation of all project components except the wastewater treatment and disposal are well advanced. Wastewater treatment and disposal of effluent through a submarine outfall to the Caribbean Sea generated opposition from various interest groups, which delayed the process of obtaining the environmental license needed in the wastewater evacuation component.

ACUACAR adopted several strategies to build consensus—a process that led to the issuance of the environmental license by the regional environmental authority. These strategies included the following:

- expansion of the participatory approach and working with the community to provide information on the impact of the outfall and its benefits (about 250 events have been carried out).
- execution of a publicity campaign on the outfall, including newspaper articles, radio and television advertisements, and the preparation and distribution of brochures.
- implementation of a social community development program, including support for urban rehabilitation, improvement of sanitary conditions, and cleanup activities; strengthening and development of community organizations to promote participation and social control; and promotion of community development to consolidate communities, prevent or reduce conflicts, and recover cultural heritage, mainly by rehabilitating the Cienaga.
- organization of a study tour for community leaders and representatives of the media, the municipality, the environmental authorities, and other stakeholders to similar outfall sites in Latin America. The group included about 30 people, who visited outfalls in Chile (Viña del Mar, Valparaiso, and Concepción); Montevideo, Uruguay; and Guaruja, Brazil. All of these outfalls are comparable in size to the outfall proposed for Cartagena and have the same type of preliminary treatment. Unlike the outfall proposed for Cartagena, all of them are located in front of the most desirable residential areas and beach resorts (in Cartagena the outfall will be about 20 kilometers north of the city). In all sites visited the outfalls are functioning successfully, to the complete satisfaction of all the local stakeholders.
- creation of a panel of five international experts (hired to review the project) with broad experience in wastewater management, design and construction of ocean outfalls, water quality, oceanographic modeling, environmental impact assessment, and private sector participation. The panel provided valuable support in clarifying technical issues to stakeholders.
- holding of a series of workshops with groups opposed to the outfall to explain the scientific, technical, and engineering aspects of the selected alternative and its advantages over all others.
- financing of participation by representatives of key stakeholders in an international course on the submarine outfall alternative for final dis-

posal of sewage for coastal cities in the Caribbean organized by the Pan-American Health Organization and the World Health Organization in Barbados in July 2002.

Implementation of these strategies took a long time. Four and a half years were required to obtain and ratify the environmental license, delaying implementation of the wastewater treatment and disposal component. Despite the delay, the project is expected to be completed by the closing date.

Guinea: Third Urban Development Project

Project Data

Project title: Third Urban Development Project (P001074)
Sector: Urban Development
Region: Sub-Saharan Africa
Country: Guinea
Cities and size of cities: Conakry, 1,767,000; secondary cities, fewer than 500,000
Sector codes: Solid waste management (23 percent), roads and highways (55 percent), subnational government administration (22 percent)
Theme codes: Municipal governance and institution building (primary), other urban development (primary), pollution management and environmental health (secondary)
Amount of loan and total project value: US$18 million, US$19.5 million
Fiscal year of approval: 1999
Scheduled closing date: June 30, 2004
Task Team Leader: Catherine D. Farvacque-Vitkovic, Lead Urban Planner, Africa Water and Urban Unit 2

Project Profile

Development objectives: The project aims to improve urban living conditions in Guinea by providing basic priority services to Conakry's urban population and by creating an enabling environment for sustained programming, financing, and management of priority investments and services in other major urban centers. In addition, it aims to reinforce the capacities of municipalities by targeting specific municipal services and by introducing new tools to improve selection and implementation of infrastructure and basic services benefiting as many people as possible.

Benefits and target population: The project aims to bring about lasting improvements in the city of Conakry in environmental health, accessibility of underserved neighborhoods, the road network, and the revenue and managerial capacity of the Governorate's financial services. It also aims to improve planning, programming, and financing of priority services and infrastructure maintenance in secondary cities.

The project is expected to reduce the incidence of diseases caused by poor sanitation and to improve the quality of urban environment through better solid waste collection and sanitary disposal. About 800,000 inhabitants are expected to benefit from improved garbage collection services and reduced exposure to sanitation-related diseases.

The provision or repair of access roads for currently inaccessible neighborhoods in Conakry will yield considerable benefits for the residents. The reduced cost and duration of trips to other areas within the city will reduce health risks, improve educational opportunities, and increase job opportunities. Within neighborhoods, it will foster the emergence of local trade and services and enhance public safety. These advantages will have the greatest impact on neighborhoods that are most inaccessible and that typically house the poorest segments of the population. The temporary hiring of jobless local residents by contractors will bring additional revenues. The construction of primary roads and rehabilitation of secondary roads will provide easier access for residents of the most populated districts of Ratoma and Matoto to the administrative and financial services located in Kaloum; increase mobility and access to urban and social services, including the Kagbelen landfill; and improve traffic fluidity among neighborhoods and between the capital, the outskirts of Conakry, and the rest of the country.

In Conakry support for increased mobilization of local authorities will involve mayors in neighborhood upgrading programs. In secondary cities mayors will make decisions on priority community improvement investments to be financed by the project.

The project is expected to create about 4,000 jobs by privatizing household garbage collection and street cleaning and promoting the use of labor-intensive trash collection techniques. It will also strengthen the managerial and marketing capacities of more than 30 small waste collection contractors. The introduction of procedures and programs for routine and periodic maintenance of secondary roads is expected to substantially increase the volume of public works that can be contracted out to small contractors in the informal sector and to consulting firms in Conakry and secondary cities.

Project description (components): The project includes four components:

- The solid waste management component aims to increase the level of garbage collection and limit the impact of waste production by operat-

ing, in a sustainable way, the La Minière landfill and setting up a landfill facility at Kagbelen.
- The neighborhood upgrading component aims to support rehabilitation and maintenance operations on Conakry's secondary roads.
- The primary road network component aims to reduce traffic at critical blockage points in Conakry.
- The institutional strengthening component aims to support operational units and improved financing of priority services, such as solid waste management and secondary road maintenance, and to finance community outreach programs related to waste management. Assistance to secondary cities supports the decentralization process by helping mayors better plan for the needs of their municipalities.

Strategic choices: This project has three objectives: to support the decentralization process by including interventions in secondary cities; to improve urban living conditions, especially in Conakry, by facilitating the population's access to basic services; and to improve the mobilization of local resources.

The financing system chosen—in which infrastructure rehabilitation is financed at a level corresponding to the borrower's previously demonstrated maintenance capacities—is expected to increase the sustainability of investments. Unlike the Second Urban Development Project (UPD2), this project targets the financing needs of solid waste management and road maintenance. However, since local tax revenues remain the primary source of financing, efforts to increase local resource mobilization continue with a more operational approach.

Institutional and implementation arrangements (counterparts): Overall project coordination is the responsibility of the Ministry of Urban Planning and Housing. The experience of UDP2 showed the need to put in place a streamlined entity charged solely with implementing the project. That entity needs to be given a single, clear mandate; a procedures manual; and an operating budget. In this project, therefore, an autonomous project unit is responsible for project accounts and administrative and financial management. To continue the considerable institutional strengthening efforts, this project unit relies on units created under UDP2 and on existing administrative structures, as follows:

- The Public Solid Waste Transfer Service, a public entity of the city of Conakry, plays a key role in setting up the solid waste management subcomponent.
- The secondary Road Maintenance Unit, created under UDP2 within the technical services of the city of Conakry, implements the neighborhood

upgrading component. It is in charge of scheduling works, preparing bidding documents, and monitoring and implementing works.

- The Urban Development Department (DATU), which received technical assistance for studies and monitoring of primary road works under UDP2, continues to perform this function and to be responsible for the primary road network component.
- The Urban Programming Unit, created under UDP2, continues to update Conakry's rapid street addressing system and implement the support to secondary cities component.
- The project unit, in close collaboration with the National Revenues Department and the financial services of the Governorate, is in charge of the component dealing with improving financing for priority services.

Institutional strengthening and technical assistance activities: Institutional strengthening consists of three main subcomponents. The first, support for operational units with a key role in implementing the project, includes assistance in logistical, financial, and human resources needed to carry out their mandates. This support includes financing expenditures (except salaries) required to maintain the continuity of the units' activities; periodic technical assistance to monitor the work of the units, guide their activities, and identify their needs; and targeted training, where needed.

The second subcomponent, support for improved financing of priority services, includes streamlining the financing system of the city, the main entity responsible for implementing priority urban services; improving the functioning of the chain of command for the collection of business and property taxes, the city's two main sources of revenue; and setting up more appropriate financial management procedures for the city and communes of Conakry in order to ensure that adequate resources are allocated to identified priority services.

The third subcomponent, community outreach program, supports an information, education, and communication campaign intended to increase awareness of the importance of signing up for garbage collection service, to explain new institutional arrangements, and to provide information on the proposed fees charged by private contractors. The program broadcasts television spots and radio announcements, sponsors sporting events and theatrical performances, conducts information sessions in schools and district-level discussions, sponsors neighborhood cleanliness contests, and holds awards celebrations honoring and encouraging small and medium-size enterprises that have recruited subscribers or demonstrated efficient management.

Urban Environmental Aspects

The project targets urban environmental goals 1 (protect and enhance environmental health in urban areas) and 2 (protect water, soil, and air quality in urban areas from contamination and pollution). Most of the loan (77 percent, or US$13.8 million) is allocated to addressing urban environmental issues.

The project integrates different urban environmental concerns, such as provision of solid waste collection services and waste disposal, neighborhood upgrading in low-income areas in Conakry, and environmental projects (storm water drainage, flood protection, school latrines with plumbing, garbage transfer points) in secondary cities.

It aims to improve urban environmental quality and protect environmental resources by investing in sanitary landfills and better waste collection services. It addresses quality-of-life issues through urban upgrading, thereby attempting to improve environmental health. These benefits cannot be measured in the absence of environmental health indicators, which the project lacks. The project does use proxy operational indicators, including the percentage of open dumps closed and the percentage of solid waste collected and disposed of in sanitary landfills.

Ongoing Implementation

The project closing date was extended in December 2002 to June 30, 2004. Progress on the action plan agreed upon at the time of the extension is satisfactory, as a result of the diligent commitment of the coordinating unit. Counterpart funding by the National Development Bank is satisfactory; loan reimbursement by the regional government and the City of Conakry, however, has experienced serious delays. The disbursement rate of the project remains low, at 35.1 percent as of March 2003, with forecasts of 82 percent by December 2003.

Component I: Infrastructure and Priority Services in Conakry

Solid waste management: The solid waste management component is progressing well. Household collection and transfer to the landfill continue to improve in terms of quantity of waste collected and transferred. As a result of the project, 31 small and medium-size enterprises had been created as of April 2003. Pending issues are renewal of contracts for waste collection and street sweeping, delays in counterpart funding for the Public Solid Waste Transfer Service, and financial monitoring of its activities. Progress indicators for this component include the following:

• Ninety percent of open dumps in Conakry have been eliminated.

- Eight-nine percent of solid waste generated in Conakry was collected and disposed of in 2002.
- Some 2,500 new jobs have been created by the small- and medium-size enterprises that collect waste in Conakry.
- Some 119,000 households have contracted the services of these enterprises to have their waste collected—more customers than those of the water and electricity utilities.

Neighborhood upgrading: Decentralized programming, complex municipal participation, and difficulties encountered in mobilizing local counterpart funding have been the main causes of delays in implementing the project. As of April 2003, the first tranche of the project was almost fully executed and the bidding documents for the second tranche had been approved.

Primary roads: The primary roads component is progressing well. The bidding documents for the preparatory works for the T7 and the Voie Express are ready, and the consultation process for the *mission de suivi et de controle* is under way. The project will also include the construction of an access road at the Gbéssia Airport, which initially was going to be funded under a now closed credit (PCPEA).

Component II: Support to Secondary Cities

As of April 2003 four municipal contracts had been signed (in Kindia, Labé, Nzérékoré, and Kankan). The contracts for Labé and Kindia are under implementation, and municipal audits (leading to municipal contracts) are being prepared in six other municipalities (Mamou, Kissidougou, Faranah, Boké, Macenta, and Siguiri). Mayors, town councils, economic operators, and community groups understand the mechanisms of the municipal contract and are very much engaged in the process of the audits and the identification of their investment and adjustment programs. Unlike in Conakry, local counterpart funding is available and timely.

Component III: Support to Financing of Priority Services and Institutional Strengthening

Following a major breakthrough on local taxation in response to a request made under this project—modification of the *clé de repartition* of the CFU (land tax) and the TPU (business tax) between central and local governments—the budgets of the city and of the five municipalities of Conakry have continued to increase.

República Bolivariana de Venezuela: Caracas Slum-Upgrading Project

Project Data

Project title: Caracas Slum-Upgrading Project (P040174)
Sector: Urban Development
Region: Latin America and the Caribbean
Country: República Bolivariana de Venezuela
City and size of city: Caracas, 3.51 million
Sector codes: General water, sanitation, and flood protection sector (52 percent); housing construction (26 percent); administration of subnational government administrations (12 percent); other social services (health, 9 percent); and finance of micro- and small and medium-size enterprises finance (1 percent)
Theme codes: Access to urban services for the poor (primary); civic engagement, participation, and community-driven development (primary)
Amount of loan and total project value: US$60.7 million, US$152.9 million
Fiscal year of approval: 1998
Scheduled closing date: June 30, 2004
Task Team Leader: Dean Cira, Senior Urban Specialist, Latin America and the Caribbean Urban Cluster

Project Profile

Development objectives: This project aims to improve the quality of life of the inhabitants of selected informal settlements (representing 15 percent of the informal settlement population) in metropolitan Caracas by developing and implementing a community-driven, sustainable, and replicable infrastructure improvement program. The project follows the general directives defined by the Plan Sectorial de Incorporación a la Estructura Urbana de las Zonas de Barrios del Area Metropolitana de Caracas y la Región Capital (Plan Sectorial). That plan, approved by the Ministry of Urban Development in 1994, outlines a comprehensive approach for improving living conditions in the informal settlements of metropolitan Caracas. The project also aims to establish a model for implementing the Plan Sectorial.

Benefits and target population: The project targets two separate agglomerations of informal settlements in Caracas: Petare Norte and La Vega. Together the two agglomerations contain 12 distinct informal settlements and a population of 184,000. Petare Norte is an agglomeration of four contiguous informal settlements, with a population of 102,000, located in the municipality of Sucre. The project targets all informal settlements in Petare Norte. La Vega is located in the municipality of Libertador.

The project is expected to provide direct benefits to the residents of Petare Norte and La Vega by responding to community priorities by improving water systems to provide minimum service of eight hours of water, seven days a week, thereby reducing risks associated with poor water service, eliminating the need to store water, and reducing water losses. It is also expected to provide properly engineered sewerage to all households, providing direct health and environmental benefits to the community; improve access to, from, and within the barrios, resulting in better circulation as well as lower transport costs for the informal settlement dwellers; improve public lighting in streets and alleyways, increasing safety; reduce the number of families living in areas of high geotectonic risk or in structurally unsound buildings; empower communities by fostering community participation and decision-making at the local level and providing support to local institutions; and improve access to housing credit through formal market channels so that families can expand or improve the physical condition of their housing units.

Project description (components): The project has three components:

- The urban upgrading component finances the design and execution of community neighborhood improvement plans for designing and executing pedestrian and vehicular access, water distribution, sewerage and sanitation, drainage, electricity distribution, public lighting, community centers, and new houses for resettlement.
- The institutional development component finances the start-up and operational costs of the project management unit, including public dissemination, monitoring and evaluation, and technical assistance and capacity building in several areas.
- The credit component supports the development and operation of a market-based loan fund that will provide housing credits to the residents of informal settlements for home improvements.

Strategic choices: The project addresses the four main factors that significantly reduce the functionality of the informal settlements: the lack of an adequate definition of property rights, the absence of collective action mechanisms to resolve the problem of providing public goods, the lack of credit to facilitate housing construction, and the integrated packaging of basic urban services.

The project aims to grant full property rights to residents of informal settlement over the sites they currently occupy. Land titling is to be done through conventional titling procedures. The sites are defined as part of the process of preparing the neighborhood improvement plans. The expectation of title is to be used as an incentive to partially recover the costs of project investments through a one-time combined levy. The transfer of title is provisional until the debt has been paid.

The project also aims to put in place collective action mechanisms by assigning the responsibility for planning, coordinating, and executing the project to a special agency, the project management unit located in the Foundation for Community Development and Municipal Promotion (FUNDACOMUN). The municipalities of Libertador and Sucre are to be strengthened so that they can support the project management unit during implementation and carry out their legal obligations with respect to the informal settlements after implementation. The project also makes full use of NGOs and community-based organizations in metropolitan Caracas for implementation aspects. Two instruments consolidate community participation efforts: local co-management groups and the neighborhood improvement plans.

Credit for housing construction in the informal settlements is facilitated by developing a privately funded and market-based program to deliver housing improvement loans to low-income populations; applying nontraditional lending methodologies to reach low-income populations; establishing a guarantee fund, to be used by participating banks, designed to demonstrate borrower capacity and willingness to pay as well as provide a hedge against macroeconomic shock risks; providing technical assistance to borrowers to ensure that they build with adequate structural integrity, target priority investments, and receive expected benefits of housing improvements; and leveraging government resources by providing access to private funding and allocating risks to those parties best able to manage or assess them.

Basic urban services are integrated by dealing simultaneously with titling; providing access to urban services; replacing housing in risk-prone areas; and providing water, sanitation and drainage, electricity, and public lighting. At the design level, coordination of the package of basic urban services is ensured through the preparation of neighborhood improvement plans by communities within each informal settlement, with help from qualified professionals where necessary. The communities bear direct responsibility for procurement and management, with help from the project management unit, or delegate this responsibility in full to the project management unit, with the community group acting in an advisory capacity. The capacity of the community is strengthened through technical assistance and empowerment.

Institutional and implementation arrangements (counterparts): FUNDACOMUN, a decentralized and semi-autonomous national public administration organization under the Ministry of Family Affairs, is the principal central government executing agency for the project, and the project is run through a project management unit located in FUNDACOMUN. The organization is responsible for the flow of project funds, including funds for project management and coordination and funds for project execution. It provides direction to the project management unit and helps establish overall policies, execution strategies, coordination, and evaluation of the project, from its inception to termination. FUNDACOMUN is assisted in its role as a strategic planner by a consultative council that includes high-level representatives from the relevant state and local governments, the Caracas Water Company, the National Housing Institute, and beneficiary communities.

The project management unit, the semi-autonomous, specialized unit responsible for coordinating, administering, and executing the project, consists of an executive management unit assisted by a technical commission. The two are responsible for the overall coordination and management of the project, including the coordination of all sources of funding. The executive management unit provides overall coordination, including maintaining relations with various institutional entities. The technical commission provides technical advice to the executive management unit and facilitates a permanent interface between the executive management unit and other institutional entities. Under the executive management unit, four separate management units are responsible for specific project tasks: the procurement and contracting administration unit, the project administration and finance unit, the physical planning–project management unit for Petare Norte, and the physical planning–project management unit for La Vega.

The physical planning–project management units for Petare Norte and La Vega coordinate and manage the technical aspects of project execution at the ground level and provide the critical interface between project execution in the field and the executive management unit. They are also responsible for managing all special programs, including resettlement, land titling, and environmental management; directing and managing the design and execution phases of the subprojects; coordinating the inspection of plans and works; and providing direct coordination with construction companies executing the works, local authorities, public utility companies, local co-management groups, and communities.

In each of the project neighborhoods, a local design office was set up at the onset of the project to serve as the primary interlocutor in developing and implementing the neighborhood improvement plans. The local design office consists of five units: the General Assembly, which approves the neighborhood improvement plans and ensures that the views of all members of the community are heard; the office of the General Director, who guarantees the effective, efficient, and equitable execution of the neighborhood improvement plans; the community participation units, which stimulate and ensure the active participation of communities in the design and execution phases of the neighborhood improvement plans; the technical assistance and social outreach unit, which assists in the technical aspects of the design and execution of the neighborhood improvement plan; and the administration unit, which monitors subproject budgets, administers the project, and maintains financial control over funds.

Institutional strengthening and technical assistance activities: The institutional development component consists of project management and municipal capacity building. The project management subcomponent financed the start-up and operational costs of the project management unit, including public dissemination, monitoring, and evaluation. It also financed a study to determine the feasibility of setting up the project management unit into an autonomous metropolitan agency, whose responsibility would be to coordinate and manage investment in the informal settlements of Caracas and handle project management responsibilities in future projects. The project also finances studies of project cost recovery and land market monitoring.

The municipal capacity building subcomponent involves developing an urban cadastral system that can serve as a planning tool for future investment in the two barrios of Petare Norte and La Vega and as the basis for more fully incorporating these and other informal settlements into the planning cadastres of the municipalities of Libertador and Sucre; establishing technical norms and standards to develop general indicators of appropriate urban design standards to be followed in urbanization projects in informal settlements; and developing financing and cost-recovery strategies to increase the municipalities' capacity to collect taxes and reduce their dependence on intergovernmental transfers.

Urban Environmental Aspects

The project targets urban environmental goals 1 (protect and enhance environmental health in urban areas) and 2 (protect water, soil, and air quality in urban areas from contamination and pollution). More than one-third of the loan amount (38 percent, or US$23 million) is allocated to addressing urban environmental issues.

The project integrates several urban environmental concerns at the neighborhood level. It combines the provision of water supply and the construction of properly engineered sewerage, to eliminate the current practice of combining surface water with household wastewater drainage, thus providing direct environmental health benefits to resident communities. By reducing the number of families living in areas at high risk of geotectonic events, the project also minimizes the potential loss of life due to natural disasters.

The project uses pollution reduction indicators (the percentage of fecal matter in sewer and drainage canals), access to services indicators (the number of legal water and sewerage connections), and proxy operational indicators (kilometers of drainage channel constructed and rehabilitated). The environmental health benefits cannot be directly measured, because the project does not provide such indicators.

Ongoing Implementation

The project's overall rating and rating on development objectives are satisfactory, but its implementation rating is unsatisfactory. The project is in its final and most critical year of execution. Dogged from the outset by a change in government, long delays in effectiveness, weak management in the early years, the natural disaster of 2000, and the national strike of 2000, the project is at least two years behind schedule.

Only about 30 percent of the works planned for 2002 were implemented. Much of the delay, especially problems in contracting and disbursements, can be attributed to the project management unit. The process of selecting consulting firms and construction firms took longer than planned, because evaluation committees were not able to meet (due to other commitments), few construction companies were interested in working in informal settlements, and FUNDACOMUN duplicated efforts of the evaluation committee.

Disbursements are also lagging. As of September 2003, only about US$8.0 million of the US$60.0 million of loan funds had been disbursed. Reasons for slow disbursement include the delay in implementation, the lack of capacity on the part of contractors and inspectors to prepare payment requests on time, the delay in requesting the Bank's no objection to additional works, the elimination of systems control, the absence of a costs engineer in the management and technical team, the national strike of 2000, and the time-consuming internal review processes. The Bank and the implementing agencies have agreed on steps to improve both procurement and disbursement.

With the 2003 investment plan, new disbursements are expected to be about US$10 million, which would mean total disbursement of US$17 million by the end of 2003. It is on this target amount that any extension decision will be based.

Nicaragua: Natural Disaster Vulnerability Reduction Project

Project Data

Project title: Natural Disaster Vulnerability Reduction Project (P064916)
Sector: Urban Development
Region: Latin America and the Caribbean
Country: Nicaragua
City and size of city: 31 secondary cities with populations of less than 500,000
Sector codes: Central government administration (67 percent), subnational government administration (26 percent), other social services (health, 7 percent)
Theme codes: Natural disaster management (primary), other social protection and risk management (primary), municipal governance and institution building (secondary)
Amount of loan and total project value: US$13.5 million, US$16.05 million
Fiscal year of approval: 2001
Scheduled closing date: March 31, 2005
Task Team Leader: Alexandra Ortiz, Senior Urban Economist, Latin America and the Caribbean Urban Cluster

Project Profile

Development objectives: This project aims to improve disaster management in Nicaragua by strengthening institutional capability in disaster management and mitigation at the national level; promoting disaster awareness and "preventive thinking" through public sector education and awareness programs; building local capacity to manage disaster emergencies, assess risk, and identify mitigation measures; and implementing vulnerability reduction and mitigation measures at the local level.

Benefits and target population: Populations at risk from natural disasters are the target beneficiaries of the project. Most groups at risk in Nicaragua are poor and live in marginal urban settlements and rural communities. The project supports emergency preparedness by ensuring the organization, training, and equipping of emergency response committees in all municipalities. The project also provides mitigation help to 25 municipalities selected as most vulnerable to natural disasters by carrying out technically supported risk assessments and vulnerability analyses and developing "preventive" land use plans and specific disaster mitigation programs. The project implements a small number of high-impact, priority mitigation measures in the 25 target municipalities. The selection process used to identify highly vulnerable municipalities included a poverty analysis and a hazard risk mapping.

Project description (components): The project consists of six components:

- *Strengthening the national system for disaster management*: This component ensures the establishment of a sustainable national system for disaster management and strengthens its capacity to respond to, prevent, and prepare for natural disasters by strengthening the institutions of the Executive Secretariat and of the national system.
- *Developing a national mitigation program and strategy*: This component aims to improve the capacity of key technical agencies involved in preparing mitigation policies and strategies. In addition to a sector coordinator to manage the component, the project finances a mitigation information system; development of a resettlement policy for homes at risk from natural disasters; strategic mitigation studies to prepare a seismic vulnerability assessment for Managua, assess watershed vulnerability, and review and update national building codes; preparation of a long-term national mitigation program and strategy; and expert technical assistance in local vulnerability analyses and identification of mitigation measures.
- *Building public awareness about disaster prevention*: This component aims to make disaster prevention a part of daily life and culture. In addition to funding a public relations expert to manage the component, the project finances mainstreaming disaster awareness into formal education, creating a public awareness program, and strengthening disaster knowledge through the media.
- *Strengthening local capacity for disaster risk management*: In addition to financing a territorial coordinator to manage this component, the project finances consolidation of committees for disaster management and the promotion of preventive planning.
- *Implementing local vulnerability reduction measures*: This component supports the Social Emergency Fund in order to develop annual operating

plans in conjunction with the territorial coordinator for municipalities participating in preventive planning. The Fund selects subprojects, prepares municipal investment plans, and implements and evaluates mitigation measures.

- *Developing administrative capacity in financial management of the project*: This component develops financial administrative capacity for procurement, contracting and acquisitions, flow of funds, disbursements, payments, internal and external auditing, and financial reporting.

Strategic choices: Three strategic choices were made at the design stage. First, the relatively short (three-year) duration of the project reflects a strategy of attending to urgent start-up needs while the national system and the Executive Secretariat are still being set up; this leaves vulnerability assessments and studies, which could lead to further support and to a possible follow-up operation. This also calls for the development of plans and studies that could lead to future activities or projects and for an evaluation of the Secretariat's performance at the beginning of the final year of the project. This evaluation should indicate whether the Executive Secretariat needs additional strengthening in disaster management, particularly in disaster preparedness and response, and whether it is ready to undertake new activities in mitigation and prevention.

Second, the project was designed to complement the work of other donors, based on careful review of the technical assistance for disaster management currently being provided to or planned for Nicaragua. The project, therefore, does not include investments in sophisticated weather and flood monitoring and early alert systems (with the exception of simple, community-managed systems) because these systems have relatively high operation and maintenance costs, and several donors, notably Finland, Spain, and the United States, have made or intend to make contributions in these areas.

Third, project coverage was defined following a careful study of vulnerability in Nicaragua's 151 municipalities and an assessment of institutional capacity within the national system. A key objective was to cover all municipalities in the country in terms of emergency preparedness and response. The complementary but more costly activities associated with prevention and mitigation are focused on the 25 most vulnerable municipalities. Coverage of the remaining municipalities could be carried out under a follow-on project or through support from other donors.

Institutional and implementation arrangements (counterparts): The Executive Secretariat for Disaster Prevention, Mitigation, and Response is responsible for overall project management and, ultimately, implementation. Within the Secretariat, project management is the direct responsibility of the Planning Department. The Planning Department is also responsible for implementing the project component on strengthening the national system for disaster management. It relies on its various units, the Secretariat's Department of Finance and Administration, and on the civil defense system to implement specific subcomponents. The remaining project components are the responsibility of different departments of the Secretariat or agencies of the national system. The Secretariat's Sector Coordination Department is responsible for developing a national mitigation program and strategy, its Public Relations Department for building public awareness of disaster prevention, and its Territorial Coordination Department for strengthening local capacity for disaster risk management; the Social Emergency Fund is responsible for implementing local vulnerability reduction measures; and the Coordinating Unit for Reform of the Public Sector (UCRESEP) is responsible for financial management of the project. These departments and agencies together form the Technical Committee for Project Implementation, headed by the Planning Department of the Executive Secretariat.

The Technical Committee prepares annual operating plans and budgets, project progress reports, and the terms of reference for contracts financed under the project, which it submits to the Planning Department of the Secretariat. The Planning Department is responsible for passing on approved operating plans, budgets, and terms of reference to UCRESEP in a timely way so that it can manage procurement and financial reporting. It is also responsible for receiving the integrated project management reports from UCRESEP, reviewing and sharing them with the World Bank and the Technical Committee, and presenting semi-annual progress reports.

Institutional strengthening and technical assistance activities: Given its development objectives, all of the project components provide institutional strengthening, capacity building, or technical assistance. They are delivered through central and local institutions in charge of disaster prevention and management; their implementation is crucial to achieving the project development objective.

Urban Environmental Aspects

The project targets urban environmental goal 4 (prevent and mitigate urban impacts of natural disasters and climate change). The entire loan amount (US$13.5 million) is allocated to preventing and mitigating the impacts of natural disasters, in both urban and rural areas.

The project uses the following output indicators: key staff of the Secretariat identified, hired, and trained by the first year of the project; new facilities for the Secretariat, including the emergency operations center, ready by the third year of the project; vulnerability studies and mitigation strategies developed for Managua and key watersheds and a review of building codes, which will lead to the development of a national disaster mitigation plan; the training of 2,000 school teachers in disaster awareness; the organization of at least 150 local disaster management committees; hazard and vulnerability assessments, identification of mitigation measures, and preventive planning activities undertaken in at least 25 eligible municipalities; mitigation measures completed in at least 15 eligible municipalities; and the preparation and identification of financing for a national disaster emergency plan by the end of project.

Ongoing Implementation

The project is rated satisfactory in terms of achievement of its development objectives. Progress is being made toward institutionalizing the National System for the Prevention, Mitigation, and Management of Disasters (SINAPRED); mainstreaming risk management at the national level; building local capacity to manage disaster emergencies; and promoting public awareness of risk management and disaster mitigation. An earthquake simulation exercise, carried out in December 2002, was a good test of the functioning of the national disaster management system. A thorough evaluation of the system highlighted weaknesses in institutional communication and coordination. Proposals for several key specialized studies, intended to expand the critical knowledge of national agencies, are being developed. Municipal disaster prevention and response committees and brigades are being trained in six municipalities. The interactive Web site, radio soap opera, and other marketing instruments are proving highly effective. Overall, there is a change in mentality at the national and local government levels as well as among citizens regarding risk and disaster management. More work is necessary to sustain this effort and improve the capabilities to respond to disaster risks and actual disasters.

The pace of project execution slowed during 2003. Delays occurred in several subcomponents, most notably in the design of the new headquarters for SINAPRED, which will also include the Center for Emergency Operations; analysis of risk and vulnerability and inclusion of preventive planning in 31 municipalities; and acquisition of equipment for 124 municipal rescue teams. Disbursements are 68 percent below plan. These delays are due to the presidential order freezing new contracts, which are needed to fill vacancies; the lack of a managerial decision regarding the reassignment of two subcomponents; and inefficiencies in the procurement processes.

Latvia: Municipal Solid Waste Management Project

Project Data

Project title: Municipal Solid Waste Management Project (P040553)
Sector: Environment
Region: Europe and Central Asia
Country: Latvia
City and size of city: Riga, 800,000
Sector codes: Solid waste management (48 percent), renewable energy (47 percent), other industry (5 percent)
Theme codes: Pollution management and environmental health (primary), access to urban services for the poor (primary)
Amount of loan, GEF grant, and total project value: US$7.95 million, US$5.12 million, US$25.2 million
Fiscal year of approval: 1999
Scheduled closing date: December 31, 2004
Task Team Leader: Anders Halldin, Senior Environmental Specialist, Europe and Central Asia Environmentally and Socially Sustainable Development Unit

Project Profile

Development objectives: This project aims to introduce modern, self-sustaining management of municipal solid waste in Latvia through the maximum sequestration of methane generated from landfills, thereby reducing greenhouse gas emissions and creating a revenue stream to cover capital and operational costs of the improved landfill. Other objectives include simplifying the separation of recyclable material, reducing environmental impacts on neighbors of the disposal site, demonstrating how outdated and obsolete disposal sites can be remediated and converted into sanitary landfills to enable continued operation, and arresting the contamination of groundwater. The project also aims to demonstrate the feasibility of developing indigenous Latvian landfill gas as an energy source and to decrease the dependence on imported fossil fuel for electricity generation and heating purposes.

Benefits and target population: Expected environmental benefits of the project include remediation of the existing Getlini site, thereby postponing the establishment of a new site located at least four times farther away; sequestration of landfill gas from already disposed waste and future waste generation, thereby reducing the emission of methane; recirculation of leachate, thereby reducing treatment costs; and demonstration of a technology that makes it possible to utilize other by-products from the decomposition of the waste, thereby prolonging the lifetime of the site and increasing the revenue stream. The project is also expected to cover its own costs, result in the cost-effective utilization of an indigenous energy resource, and produce foreign exchange savings by reducing demand for fossil fuel for heating purposes.

Project description (components): The project finances the following activities:

- remediation of the existing disposal site in Getlini
- introduction of technical and operational improvements to meet European Union sanitary landfill standards
- establishment of a sorting line for separating recyclable materials and arranging separate areas for the storage of separated material as well as hazardous waste to be later transported to another site
- establishment of a modern waste management technology based on energy cells for enhanced degradation of easily biodegradable waste
- collection of landfill gas containing about 50 percent methane
- site generation of electricity by gas engines, with direct delivery to the grid
- provision of technical assistance through twinning arrangements to enable the staff of the disposal site to efficiently operate the waste processing system and to achieve maximum revenues from the generated landfill gas and separated by-products
- provision of managerial assistance during the implementation period to facilitate the future development of Getlini-Eco Limited (GLE)

These activities are grouped into three integrated investment components and one technical assistance component: remediation of the existing site to meet environmental requirements regarding leachate treatment and prevent future groundwater contamination; technical and operational improvements to meet European Union sanitary landfill standards and arrangements for improving the separation of recyclable materials; establishment of energy cells for enhanced degradation of easily biodegradable waste, collection of landfill, and generation of electricity; and technical and managerial assistance through appropriate twinning arrangements.

URBANENVIRONMENT AND INFRASTRUCTURE

Strategic choices: The project was originally a component of the Municipal Services Development Project (Loan 34584-LV 1995). Because identification of a new disposal site would have delayed the finalization and implementation of that project, this component was developed as a separate project.

The original project concept was based on the development of a new location for the future management of Riga's waste, given preliminary indications that the groundwater was threatened by the leachate emanating from the Getlini disposal site. However, a 1996–97 study financed by the Swedish government found that the contamination of the groundwater was limited to the shallowest Quaternary aquifer; the more important and deeper aquifers, the Plavinas and Amata (used as resources for the water supply to Riga) had not been contaminated. The study forecast that the Plavinas aquifer would show signs of contamination about 2002 and the Amata aquifer would do so about 2020. It concluded, however, that the project could prevent additional risks of leachate contamination of the water supply. The study also indicated that operation of the Getlini site could continue for another 50 years if the proposed technology were implemented as planned. With further utilization of by-products, the lifetime of the site would be 100–200 years. The study concluded that investments based on the collection of landfill gas to generate electricity would provide a cost-effective and sustainable solution to the current waste management problem for Riga.

In view of the large number of disposal sites that need to be either remediated and closed or remediated for continued operation, Latvia has an important investment program ahead. Given that improved waste management normally results in a substantial increase in the disposal fee, the development of improved waste management will need to be phased in to make the changes affordable. This project allows the site to meet Western sanitary landfill standards without increasing disposal fees. It demonstrates a replicable technology and deals with the current waste management problems in a cost-effective way.

Rationale for involvement of the Global Environment Facility (GEF) and other donors: The project is consistent with the guidance for accessing the short-term climate change window of the GEF operational strategy in that it is technically, environmentally, and socially sustainable; it is a national priority in the National Climate Change Mitigation Plan (1995) as well as in the Environmental National Policy Plan; it provides the means of abating greenhouse gas emissions at a cost of US$3.41 per ton of carbon, far below the maximum acceptable costs of US$10 per ton carbon; it includes an essential transfer of technology through twinning arrangements and managerial assistance during project implementation; and it develops the emission of methane, a potent greenhouse gas, into an indigenous energy resource. In addition, the project provides a mechanism for the GEF to support the development of a cost-effective waste management technology as a means of reducing greenhouse gas emissions. If successfully implemented, the project could serve as a paradigm for most of the municipalities in the Baltic region, all of which must improve the management of solid waste. The high potential for reducing greenhouse gas emissions led the GEF Council to approve a grant equivalent of US$5.12 million.

The Swedish International Development Agency (SIDA) has declared its willingness to support the project with a US$1.5 million investment grant. Its funding rationale is its belief that the project will eliminate the ongoing discharge of untreated leachate and polluted runoff water from the Getlini site to the River Daugava, a tributary of the Baltic Sea. Cleanup of the Baltic Sea has become an environmental priority for Sweden.

Institutional and implementation arrangements (counterparts): The Riga City Council has overall responsibility for the project, through a steering committee. While the city council supervises implementation, realization of the investments is delegated to the new company, GLE. The company has a management structure that facilitates the remediation efforts of the existing landfill and allows it to oversee the production of landfill gas. Actual operation of the landfill is delegated to the external contractor through a management contract.

To assist with procurement and disbursements, a project procurement unit was set up as a separate unit within the Riga City Council, under a unit head who reports directly to the chair of the project steering committee. To help the steering committee supervise implementation during the first two years, an international and a local project adviser were hired. Their role is to make sure that all necessary documents are prepared and that the permits required to maintain the project's implementation schedule are obtained.

The technical assistance required for physical project implementation is being provided through twinning arrangements under the SIDA grant. The twinning agreement provides expertise to both GLE and the company contracted for operation of the energy cells.

Institutional strengthening and technical assistance activities: The project finances technical and operational improvements to meet Western sanitary landfill standards; technical assistance through twinning arrangements to enable the staff of the disposal site to efficiently operate the waste processing system and to achieve maximum revenues from the generated landfill gas and separated by-products; and managerial assistance during implementation to facilitate the future development of GLE.

Urban Environmental Aspects

The project targets urban environmental goal 3 (minimize the urban impact on natural resources at regional and global scales). Its entire loan and grant amount is allocated to addressing urban environmental issues. The project takes an integrated approach to solid waste management, including segregation of recyclable and other waste, reutilization of outdated and obsolete waste disposal sites, introduction of modern waste management technology, collection of landfill gas, and generation of electricity. The project demonstrates a cost-effective and sustainable solution to the waste management problem in Riga and reduces greenhouse gas emissions. It thus improves the local environment by reducing groundwater pollution, surface water pollution, dust and air pollution caused by fires, noise from activities on the site, and odors from uncovered waste material. In addition, it reduces imports of fossil fuels by generating 6 megawatts of power and reduces greenhouse gas emissions, at a cost of US$3.41 per ton of carbon. The project also substantially improves the working conditions for people involved in separating and recycling waste material.

As a pollution reduction indicator, it uses the amount of methane captured, setting a goal of at least 13 million Nm^3/year (cubic meters of methane) as of 2001. It also monitors the quality of groundwater on a yearly basis. Monthly data are collected on separated waste and on temporarily stored hazardous waste.

Ongoing Implementation

The implementation of the project began in September 2000; the collection of landfill gas and generation of electricity, which was supposed to have begun in early 2002, was delayed to the end of 2002 because of contractual disputes between GLE and the buyer Latvenergo. At that time, the project was generating somewhat less electricity from the existing and covered landfill than initially expected. To enable a full evaluation of the project's results, the amount of gas produced in each energy cell, as well as the amount of electricity generated, is being closely monitored. The first energy cell was expected to start generating gas and electricity in mid-2003. Given the long delays experienced at the outset, the project has been extended by 18 months, to December 31, 2004.

As of June 2003, Latvenergo had agreed to pay a higher price for electricity, and management had agreed to implement the project by the new deadline and within the available project budget.

The project is expected to reduce the emission of carbon dioxide equivalents by an average 233,900 tons a year during its lifetime of 25 years. The project has started to collect landfill gas from the existing landfill and to produce electricity based on the methane content in the gas. Collection from the existing landfill is consistent with forecasted volumes, but it is too early to predict if this situation is stable. If so, the project's environmental benefits would be greater than the forecasted amount of reduced global emissions. When the project was approved for GEF financing, the conversion factor for methane to carbon dioxide was 18. Currently, it is 21, and it is expected to be corrected to 25. Environmental benefits are expected to increase 17–39 percent if the gas yield is in line with appraisal estimates.

Algeria: Industrial Pollution Control Project

Project Data

Project title: Industrial Pollution Control Project (P004960)
Sector: Environment
Region: Middle East and North Africa
Country: Algeria
City and size of city: Annaba, 465,000
Sector codes: Petrochemicals and fertilizers (45 percent), other industry (42 percent), central government administration (13 percent)
Theme codes: Pollution management and environmental health (primary), environmental policies and institutions (primary), decentralization (secondary), legal institutions for a market economy (secondary)
Amount of loan and total project value: US$78 million, US$118.1 million (project amended in August 2002; new loan amount is US$36.4 million)
Fiscal year of approval: 1996
Scheduled closing date: June 30, 2005
Task Team Leader: Hocine Chalal, Senior Environmental Specialist, Middle East and North Africa Rural Development, Water and Environment Group

Project Profile

Development objectives: This project aims to help reduce exposure to hazardous pollution that causes health problems and serious ecological degradation. It seeks to strengthen the institutional and legal framework and initiate an investment program in the industrial sector of Annaba for mitigating the adverse environmental and health effects of pollution.

Benefits and target population: The pilot investments under the project are expected to produce several major benefits. The local population of Annaba will receive relief from pollution, with positive impacts on the quality of their lives, particularly of children, who represent 40 percent of the population. From a public expenditure point of view, the project is expected to reduce health costs, with additional savings on education, workers' compensation, productivity losses, and special interventions related to pollution accidents. The Entreprise Nationale des Engrais et Produits Phytosanitaires (ASMIDAL) and the Entreprise Nationale de Sidérurgie (ENSIDER) in Annaba, although not the primary focus of the project, benefit from improvements in energy efficiency, production efficiency, and product quality, which will reduce worker exposure, improve management, and increase safety.

The concentration of pollutants in ambient air is also expected to decrease following mitigation actions. The decrease will be most prominent at point sources, but concentrations will decline throughout the region. Modeling based on the proposed mitigation measures forecasts average reductions of 45 percent for particulates, 65 percent for sulfur dioxide, 10 percent for ammonia, 25 percent for volatile organic compounds, and 5 percent for nitrogen oxides.

The project is expected to have positive social impacts by reducing exposure of the local population to industrial pollution. The villages of El-Bouni and Sidi-Ammar, which are exposed to significant industrial pollution sources, are among the lowest-income groups in the Annaba region. The project can significantly improve the welfare of these people.

Project description (components): The project consists of two components. The first focuses on strengthening the institutional and legal framework through institution building, enhancement of the legal and regulatory framework, design and implementation of a system for monitoring and enforcement, and activation of the National Environmental Fund. The second component—pilot investments—covers environmental investments at the ASMIDAL fertilizer complex and the ENSIDER iron and steel complex.

The project was restructured in 2002 and the loan agreement amended in August 2002. Nondisbursed amounts for the ENSIDER and ASMIDAL components were canceled at the request of the beneficiaries. ENSIDER was being privatized and the new owners remained committed to the project objectives. ASMIDAL was doing well financially and could obtain attractive financing from other sources. The two companies entered into a voluntary agreement with the Ministry of Environment, signing an environmental performance contract affirming their commitment to the project's objectives.

The opportunity provided by the restructuring of the project was used to reintroduce a new component, the installation of a hazardous waste treatment facility. This component had been partially appraised but then left out of the project because of the government's commitment to finance it with its own resources.

The ASMIDAL subcomponent aims to reduce sulfur dioxide, nitrogen oxides, and dust emissions (phosphate, ammonium nitrate) into the atmosphere and to eliminate phosphogypsum discharges. Major investments include the following:

- closure, demolition, and decontamination of the sulfuric and phosphoric acid plants and the import during the first year of phosphoric acid or monoammonium phosphate to compensate for the production losses resulting from the decline in activity at the two plants
- rehabilitation of Annaba's port facility to allow it to import and store raw materials for ASMIDAL
- rehabilitation of the gas treatment system in the nitric acid plant nitrate unit
- installation of a scrubber or granulator at the ammonium nitrate plant
- rehabilitation of the granulation units for the production of nitrogen-phosphate-potassium and tri-superphosphate fertilizers
- provision of technical assistance and training for plant operation and for improving workers' health and safety and the purchase of spare parts

The first, second, third, fifth, and sixth of these subcomponents had been completed when the project was restructured. Since then, the company has essentially completed the other subcomponents using its own resources.

The ENSIDER subcomponent aims to reduce emission of dusts, ammonia, and volatile organic compounds in the atmosphere and to reduce industrial discharges into the Seybouse River. Major investments include the following:

- installation or rehabilitation of dust removal systems for the electric arc furnace, sintering plants, and blast furnaces and installation of a door cleaning system in the coke ovens
- construction of two wastewater treatment plants, one for the blast furnace and one for general wastewater
- installation of a boiler for distilling ammonia
- renovation of the biological wastewater treatment plant
- establishment of an environmental laboratory for pollution monitoring
- purchase of spare parts
- institutional strengthening

Only the third and seventh subcomponents were completed before project restructuring.

Strategic choices: Three alternatives were considered for project design: a technical assistance project for strengthening the institutional and legal framework in industrial pollution, a comprehensive investment project to control industrial pollution on a national scale, and an institution-building project supplemented by a limited number of investment-related activities for addressing the most urgent and critical industrial pollution problems. The first two options were considered premature because Algeria does not have the human or financial resources to monitor and control industrial pollution on a national scale. The third option was found to be the most feasible, since it would ensure government ownership by strengthening the institutional and legal framework, focusing on those environmental investments that have a large environmental externality to justify immediate intervention.

The General Direction of the Environment (DGE) of the Ministry of Interior, Local Government and the Environment is the implementing agency for the project. Since its preparation, the project has been coordinated by an interministerial committee for coordination and follow-up. That committee is chaired by DGE and includes representatives of the ministries of health, finance, industry, and petroleum and the National Planning Council. The committee provides overall policy guidance, reviews work programs, and resolves interministerial implementation issues relating to the project. A project implementation unit, with a full-time project manager and competent technical and administrative staff, was established within DGE. The project implementation unit is responsible for interfacing between the Bank and DGE. It assists DGE in the day-to-day management of the institutional and legal component, reviews and approves the agreements signed between companies and institutions, and coordinates the implementation of the different investment subcomponents.

The pilot investment component of the project is managed by the beneficiary enterprises, in close cooperation with DGE and the Regional Environment Department. On the basis of the audits performed, least-cost mitigating plans were prepared with the appropriate package of investments, training, and technical assistance. Each enterprise was required to prepare two documents. The first was a subsidiary loan agreement, to be negotiated and signed with the Treasury. The second was an agreement to be signed with DGE that included the pollution levels authorized, as well as the monitoring and reporting requirements that ASMIDAL and ENSIDER had to fulfill. Each enterprise is responsible for its own procurement. DGE and its project implementation unit maintain regular contacts with each enterprise and ensure adherence to its implementation and procurement plans.

Institutional strengthening and technical assistance activities: Strengthening the institutional and legal framework is expected to increase capacity for policy formulation, monitoring, and enforcement. This added capacity will increase public expenditures to some degree, but it should yield major benefits in terms of substantially lowering the current social cost of environmental and natural resource degradation, keep future costs in check, and reduce the inefficiencies of the country's fragmented system of environmental protection.

Institution building: This subcomponent aims to strengthen the technical and administrative capacity of four bodies: (1) the High Council of the Environment and Sustainable Development, as the cross-sectoral forum for environmental policies; both subcommissions of the Council that oversee and review the National Environmental Action Plan; (2) DGE, the national environmental agency responsible for national policies, preparation of the National Environmental Action Plan, proposals for legislation, and ensuring operational and technical cooperation; (3) the Ministry of Industry and Restructuring, the Ministry of Health, and the National Planning Council in their environmental assessment and audit preparation, health risk assessment, and environmental planning; and (4) the Regional Environment Departments of Annaba, Skikda, Constantine, Algiers, and Oran in their monitoring and enforcement activities. This subcomponent also finances the promotion and introduction of clean technology.

Enhancement of the legal and regulatory framework: This subcomponent provides the government of Algeria with the administrative, managerial, and technical tools to review, update, and modify the most important legal texts and regulations derived from the framework environmental law and to eliminate overlaps and contradictions; apply the modified environmental assessment decree as an effective policy instrument and to develop the appropriate procedures and sector guidelines; to issue and adopt the modified decrees for the classified industrial establishments, by issuing environmental permits, by providing training and technical assistance for handling the transport of hazardous waste, and by other means; and to conduct a study of environmental liabilities.

Design and implementation of a system for monitoring and enforcement: This subcomponent aims to design and implement the environment permit system on a pilot basis in Annaba and Skikda. The permit sets a ceiling on the amount of pollution that each establishment is allowed to discharge in a given medium by establishing local environmental guidelines. It also establishes a program for reducing the total pollution load over a specific period, consistent with the technology used and the financial status of each establishment. With this subcomponent, DGE and the corresponding Regional Environment Department are expected to monitor pollution contracts and test a series of enforcement measures and financial incentives to mitigate pollution in an integrated manner.

Activation of the National Environmental Fund: This subcomponent aims to make the National Environmental Fund operational and then expand its role into an effective instrument of environmental financing as an Environmental Clean-up and Protection Fund. These activities are supported by the implementation of related studies.

Urban Environmental Aspects

The project targets urban environmental goals 2 (protect water, soil, and air quality in urban areas from contamination and pollution) and 3 (minimize the urban impact on natural resources at regional and global scales). Its entire loan amount (US$78 million) is allocated to addressing urban environmental issues.

To mitigate the adverse environmental and health impacts of pollution, the project takes a comprehensive approach to controlling industrial pollution that includes strengthening institutions, putting in place a legal framework, and investing in pilot programs. It focuses on the fertilizer complex and the iron and steel complex at Annaba, aiming to achieve measurable impacts in terms of reduced pollutants, increased energy efficiency with concomitant production efficiency, and improvements in health. All of these measures reduce public expenditure on health.

The project uses a quality of life indicator (reduction in perceived respiratory morbidity in El Bouni and Sidi Amar) and pollution reduction indicators (reduction in particulates, sulfur dioxide, ammonia, volatile organic compounds, and nitrogen oxides). An ongoing assessment, from a cost-benefit analysis point of view, looks into the program's effects in the Annaba region, where the main benefits are improved public health and improved coastal sea water quality.

Ongoing Implementation

Progress on development objectives is rated satisfactory. The expected disbursement level at the end of fiscal 2003 was US$21.7 million, or 59.3 percent. The institutional and regulatory strengthening component is also progressing, with the supply and installation of laboratory equipment and the continuation of the technical assistance component. The new component related to the design, construction, and start-up of a hazardous waste landfill is also progressing, albeit with delays.

The equipment acquired for the air quality monitoring networks in Annaba and Algiers is performing satisfactorily. The air quality in Annaba improved following the abatement of pollution from the ENSIDER and ASMIDAL industrial complexes. The project is completing a health study to assess respiratory morbidity in the area. The benefits to human health and to the ecology of the natural marine ecosystem in the Bay of Annaba, measured in monetary terms and compared with the costs of the project, will also be estimated.

Kenya, Tanzania, and Uganda: Lake Victoria Environmental Management Project

Project Data

Project title: Lake Victoria Environmental Management Project (P046837)
Sector: Environment
Region: Sub-Saharan Africa
Country: Kenya, Tanzania, and Uganda
City and size of cities: In Kenya: Kisumu, 275,000; Webuye, 47,000. In Tanzania: Mwanza, 300,000; Bukoba, 43,000. In Uganda: Kampala, 1.4 million; Jinja, 89,000
Sector codes: Central government administration (25 percent); general water, sanitation, and flood protection sector (20 percent); other social services (20 percent); tertiary education (10 percent); animal production (25 percent)
Theme codes: Biodiversity (primary), water resources management (primary), pollution management and environmental health (primary), environmental policies and institutions (primary)
Amount of loan, GEF grant, and total project value: US$35 million, US$35 million, US$77.6 million
Fiscal year of approval: 1996
Scheduled closing date: June 30, 2004, for Tanzania and Uganda; December 31, 2004, for Kenya
Task Team Leader: Richard Kaguamba, Senior Natural Resources Management Specialist, Africa Environmentally and Socially Sustainable Development Unit 2

Project Profile

Development objectives: This comprehensive project aims to rehabilitate the lake ecosystem for the benefit of the people who live in the catchment area, the countries in which they live, and the global community. The program objectives are to maximize the sustainable benefits to riparian communities from using resources within the basin to generate food, employment, and income; supply safe water; and sustain a disease-free environment. It also aims to conserve biodiversity and genetic resources for the benefit of the riparian communities and the global community. In addressing the tradeoffs among these objectives, which cut across national boundaries, the project also aims to harmonize national management programs in order to reverse, to the maximum extent possible, the increasing environmental degradation.

Benefits and target population: The main economic benefits of the project derive from avoiding the losses that can be expected if effective action is not taken. Potential benefits include expansion of artisan fishing and processing, reduction in post-harvest fish losses, implementation of water hyacinth control, conservation of wetlands, improved pasture management, conservation of catchment soil, extension of rural water and sanitation, upgrading of urban sewerage, and abatement of industrial pollution.

Project description (components): The project is the first phase of a longer-term program that provides the necessary information to improve management of the lake ecosystem; establish mechanisms for cooperative management by the three countries; and identify and demonstrate practical, self-sustaining remedies, while simultaneously building capacity for ecosystem management. The project consists of two broad sets of activities. The first set of activities, which are designed to address specific environmental threats, takes place in a series of selected pilot zones. The second set of activities, which improves information on the lake and builds capacity for more effective management, is of necessity lakewide in scope.
   The project supports the following components:

• improvements in fisheries management
• research on fisheries
• development and enforcement of extension policies on fisheries
• establishment of a fish levy trust
• introduction of water hyacinth control
• management of water quality and ecosystems
• management of industrial and municipal waste management
• improvements in land use and wetlands management
• development of an institutional framework

   The industrial and municipal waste management component forms an interface between water resources management and urban environmental activities. With a budget of US$9.89 million, this component aims to improve the management of industrial and municipal effluents and assess the contribution of urban runoff to lake pollution so that alleviation measures can be designed. Component activities are expected to prepare inventories and classifications for all factories and industries in the catchment area, assess treatment of effluent before discharge and its dilution and dispersion levels in receiving water bodies, quantify pollution and nutrient flows from urban runoff, identify and characterize pollution hot spots, formulate guidelines and effluent discharge standards, establish training arrangements for industrialists and local authorities, launch a public awareness campaign, and initiate pilot treatment projects in selected municipalities and industries. Three pilot projects are also included:

- The pilot industrial effluent treatment aims to create wetlands to test tertiary treatment through filtration of industrial waste from various sources, such as the Pan Paper Mill in Webuye (Kenya), before it discharges into the Nzoia River; from industries in Mwanza (Tanzania); and from industries in Jinja (Uganda).
- The pilot municipal effluent treatment supports the creation of wetlands to test tertiary treatment through filtration of municipal waste in Kisumu (Kenya), Mwanza (Tanzania), and Jinja (Uganda).
- Priority waste management investments include urgent rehabilitation or extension of urban sanitation systems that are currently discharging untreated waste directly into the lake. Under this subcomponent the project rehabilitates the wastewater treatment works in Kisumu (Kenya), constructs a community-based simplified sewage scheme in a portion of Mwanza (Tanzania) to complement the expansion of the water supply system financed by the European Union, improves a sludge disposal site in Bukoba (Tanzania), helps the National Water and Sewerage Corporation in Uganda develop a long-term pollution reduction strategy, and modifies the main effluent discharge into the lake at the Bugolobi treatment works in Kampala (Uganda) to increase the detention time of effluent and reduce pollution entering the lake.

Strategic choices: Lake Victoria is an international water body that is of great economic value to the three riparian countries and of great scientific and cultural significance to the global community, mainly because of its unique biodiversity.

The lake and its catchment area suffer from severe urban and rural population pressures. Environmental problems include pollution hot spots, pollution caused from the inflow of chemical residues from agriculture, heavy metals concentrations from certain industries, and the inflow of nutrients from human waste (especially untreated sewage) and soil erosion. The project locates and quantifies these problems, identifies the sources of nutrients and pollutants, undertakes ameliorative measures, and strengthens existing institutions to sustain solutions over the longer term.

Developing a framework for concerted action: Attempts at collaboration over fisheries by Kenya, Tanzania, and Uganda go back as far as 1928. Various organizations and coordinating mechanisms were created, but the lack of a strong intergovernmental mechanism for harmonizing such measures made it difficult to establish them on a lakewide basis. To facilitate such measures, this project supports the establishment of the Lake Victoria Fisheries Organization. The project ensures that management of regional fisheries management establishes, for the first time, a regional framework for environmental action rather than just commercial activities.

Urgent attention is required, through regional cooperation and a regional management framework, to address environmental issues affecting the Lake Victoria basin. Discussions to broaden cooperation led to a tripartite agreement in 1994 for jointly preparing and implementing a Lake Victoria Environmental Management Program. The essential soundness of this agreement and its main institutional arrangements worked well during project preparation. The agreement also constitutes a framework for action that is fully responsive to the requirements of a strategic action plan that identifies and analyzes transboundary water-related environmental concerns and expresses determination to jointly build the capacity of existing institutions and establish new ones for adopting a comprehensive approach to addressing shared transboundary concerns.

There have been several donor-supported initiatives in and around Lake Victoria, including those addressing priority environmental concerns. Most of these were small, uncoordinated, and incomplete, and they seldom addressed issues in an informed manner with wider environmental priorities in mind. Although often successful in their own terms, these smaller projects could have achieved even more by being part of a coordinated management initiative to address the problems of the lake ecosystem. The Lake Victoria Environmental Management Project is such a management initiative. It is expected to have an enormous impact on improving understanding of the ecosystem and helping policymakers devise sustainable management strategies.

The project—especially its wetlands component—builds on the GEF–funded Institutional Support for the Protection of East African Biodiversity project. It provides the information and builds the capacity required to coordinate the substantial investments likely to be available for financing direct actions to reduce nutrient inflows from human waste, decrease soil erosion, clean up industrial effluent, and reduce pollution. The Lake Victoria Environmental Management Project is thus seen as the essential first step in a long-term program for restoring and sustaining the ecological foundations for economic development in the lake basin and its catchment areas.

Rationale for GEF involvement: As one of the world's largest unique fresh-water biodiversity habitats, Lake Victoria was a clear candidate for GEF assistance under its operational strategy for international waters. That strategy addresses degradation of water quality due to pollution from land-based activities; introduction of nonindigenous species; excessive exploitation of living resources, leading to potentially irreversible environmental damage; hardship to the poor; and serious health concerns. With poverty endemic to the region and many competing claims for scarce development resources, the case for GEF support to develop a concerted corrective action for the environmental management of Lake Victoria was extremely strong.

Institutional and implementation arrangements (counterparts): The three project coordination offices (one in each country) established during project preparation continue their coordination role during project implementation. The Secretariats serve as the day-to-day central contact points and information clearinghouses for the implementing agencies in their respective countries and for all donors supporting the program, gathering information from the implementing agencies, monitoring the project, and preparing progress reports. A Regional Policy and Steering Committee serves as the body for overall program coordination and resolution of any possible disputes. The Lake Victoria Fisheries Organization coordinates those components associated with fisheries, although implementation is the responsibility of the individual national agencies.

Implementation of the industrial and municipal waste management program is led by the Ministry of Land Reclamation, and the Ministry of Regional and Water Development (Kenya), the Ministry of Water (Tanzania), and the Directorate of Water Development of the Ministry of Natural Resources (Uganda). They collaborate with municipal and local councils and with industry in all three countries; with the Ministry of Commerce and Industry, the Lake Basin Development Authority, and the Moi University School of Environmental Studies in Kenya; with the University of Dar es Salaam in Tanzania; and with the National Water and Sewerage Corporation and Makarere University in Uganda.

Community participation—including the empowerment of communities to assume ownership of the programs targeted for their benefit—is considered key to the successful implementation of the program. The project therefore aims to ensure that the processes of education, communication, awareness creation, and community participation and motivation are followed consistently and thoroughly throughout implementation.

Institutional strengthening and technical assistance activities: The project emphasizes capacity building and technical assistance. An estimated

20 percent of project costs are directed toward various studies, and another 42 percent go toward capacity building. Almost all components contain a mixture of information gathering, capacity building, training, equipment, and personnel support.

The Lake Victoria Environmental Management Project Secretariat coordinates capacity building programs and is responsible for training. Each implementing department and agency prepares an annual training plan and submits it to its national Secretariat. The training plan includes details on subjects and courses, timing, duration, estimated costs, names and locations of the institutions, names of the people proposed, and the justification for training. The training program includes regional fellowships, study tours, and on-site training for national, regional, and field staff; selected community leaders; fishers; farmers; and entrepreneurs.

To address the variations in implementation capacity from country to country and agency to agency, every subprogram makes extensive provision for capacity building. Provision is made for more than 2,000 short-term and on-the-job training courses, and at least 600 stakeholder workshops. The project finances the costs of master's-level courses for 100 students and of PhD courses for 15 students. Care is taken to strike a balance in the training and its timing so that enough people are available to implement the project.

The component for the riparian universities strengthens facilities for environmental analysis and graduate teaching at the Moi University School of Environmental Studies, at the University of Dar es Salaam, and at Makarere University. The project has also financed technical assistance to undertake several studies covering pollution disaster, fish biology and biodiversity conservation, sedimentation, wetlands sustainability, fisheries management, and other issues. Postgraduate students from the three universities are conducting research under this project (the pilot experiments with artificial wetlands are being carried out as student research studies, for example).

The project is financing vehicles and boats; offices; laboratory and field equipment; laboratory chemicals and reagents; construction of artificial wetlands; feasibility studies and structures for sanitation; training, workshops, and demonstrations; technical assistance; personnel costs; and operation and maintenance expenditures.

Urban Environmental Aspects

The project targets urban environmental goals 2 (protect water, soil, and air quality in urban areas from contamination and pollution) and 3 (minimize the urban impact on natural resources at the regional and global scales). Thirteen percent of the total project cost (US$9.89 million) is allocated to addressing urban environmental issues, 90 percent of which is financed by the Bank.

The project makes use of pollution reduction indicators, namely, reductions in the nutrient and fecal coliform counts from towns bordering the lake and reductions in sediment and phosphorus loading in rivers flowing into the lake. It also uses environment-related output indicators, including reductions in significant industrial pollutants entering the lake of at least 50 percent over five years, a measurable reduction in the infestation of water hyacinth, and stabilization of areas retained as wetlands.

Ongoing Implementation

The project is a multisector and regional initiative on a scale not attempted in the region since the first East African Community collapsed almost 30 years ago. The development objectives of the project were designed to reestablish regional cooperation to deal with a variety of important ecological, economic, and social problems.

Project performance has continued to be satisfactory in Tanzania and in Uganda. Kenya has had difficulty implementing the project. As a result of prolonged government bureaucracy, the flow of funds to the project has been very problematic. Procurement of goods and services needed by the project has been considerably delayed. World Bank financing for the Kenya program ended in December 2002. GEF financing was extended to close in December 2004. The GEF grant for Tanzania closed in December 2002 and is 100 percent disbursed. The World Bank credit was extended and will now close in June 2004. Supplemental World Bank financing of US$5 million was successfully negotiated and is now effective.

Following excellent implementation performance, the project task team has rated the project highly satisfactory for its Tanzania component. Results include the following:

- Water hyacinth control activities have achieved 90 percent of the target in controlling the weed.
- The fish quality laboratory is functioning well.
- Water transport equipment (vessels, boats, and other equipment) is in place and functioning.
- The water quality monitoring network was established and is functioning.
- Basin-wide land cover/use mapping and erosion hazard potential mapping has been completed.
- Biodiversity and limnology are being monitored.
- Some 511 beach management units have been established.

- Terrestrial and aquatic data collection and monitoring programs necessary to provide information needed for sensible management decisions have been initiated.
- An object-oriented approach to problem-solving has been introduced.
- Strong regional collaboration and cooperation by scientists and managers to address lakewide problems have begun.
- Institutions and the staff working in them have been strengthened to achieve a critical mass of resources needed to manage lake basin resources.
- Tools needed to undertake multidimensional management of the lake basin have been developed.
- Local communities, NGOs, community-based organizations, and local, regional, and national governments have been engaged in comanaging the natural resources of the basin.

The Bank and the government of Tanzania have agreed that the remaining year of the project will be used to consolidate the gains achieved to date. Uncompleted works will be completed, results will be documented, information will be disseminated and data collected, the application of all resource management strategies developed will be intensified, fish quality standards will be maintained and improved, and biodiversity monitoring will be continued.

Preparation of the Lake Victoria Environmental Management Project II has begun. A stocktaking exercise is being conducted to inform the preparatory process for the new project. Its findings should help improve measurement of performance indicators.

The project is completing the acquisition of critical scientific knowledge and information and consolidating the human resources and skills developed over the project period. By 2003 all outstanding procurement actions had been completed, 90 percent of those enrolled in graduate training had completed their studies and returned to duty stations, 15 manuscripts had been prepared for publication, and most of the data and reports had been copied onto CDs for safekeeping. A Web site for the project in Tanzania containing important information on the management plan has been updated. The project has been participating in global forums for exchange of knowledge and experiences.

Poland: Krakow Energy Efficiency Project

Project Data

Project title: Krakow Energy Efficiency Project (P065059)
Sector: Energy
Region: Europe and Central Asia
Country: Poland
Cities and size of cities: Krakow, 783,000; Skawina, 24,000
Sector codes: District heating and energy efficiency services (100 percent)
Theme codes: Climate change (primary), pollution management and environmental health (secondary)
Amount of loan and total project value: US$15 million, US$78.4 million
Fiscal year of approval: 2001
Scheduled closing date: December 31, 2007
Task Team Leader: Peter Johansen, Senior Energy Specialist, Europe and Central Asia Infrastructure and Energy Services Department

Project Profile

Development objectives: This project aims to improve the energy efficiency of the heating systems in the Krakow region by continuing the modernization of the district heating systems (a municipal service), helping consumers decrease their heat energy consumption by improving the energy efficiency at the end-user level, and developing the knowledge and mechanisms necessary for financiers to fund end-user energy efficiency projects.

The loan is planned to be complemented by a US$11 million GEF grant intended to remove barriers to market-oriented transactions and increase public and private sector investments in energy efficiency in buildings. The GEF contribution is planned to include both guarantee and grant facilities.

Benefits and target population: The project benefits include a more efficient and cost-effective supply of heat in the Krakow region; lower and more affordable energy bills; enhanced comfort in public, residential, and commercial buildings; better local air quality; and reduction in greenhouse gas emissions.

The direct project beneficiaries are the customers of the Municipal District Heating Enterprise (MPEC) in Krakow. They are expected to benefit from a more efficient district heating network, with lower operating costs, better service, and controllable heat use. Spillover benefits will affect all Krakow residents as the environment improves. State and municipal authorities are also expected to benefit, as a result of the improvement in the quality and delivery of district heating. Energy service company (ESCO) financing mechanisms would relieve the state and municipal budgets from upfront capital investments and reduce future operating budgets.

All residents of the region will benefit from the reduced environmental impacts of more efficient energy services to buildings in the region. Poland as a whole will also benefit from the country's reduced contribution to global greenhouse gas emissions.

ESCO activity will develop the skills of local engineers and contractors in energy management retrofitting. If the ESCO process is successful, its procedures, coupled with local commercial bank financing of new energy conservation investments through joint ventures, could be disseminated throughout Poland.

Project description (components): The project consists of three components: district heating modernization, ESCO financing, and technical assistance. The first component replaces old, inefficient, and outdated equipment with new, more efficient models of boilers, lights, motors, and other equipment in order to improve hot water distribution. The second component finances energy-saving capital investments (principally goods, materials, and installation works). The third component provides external consulting services to support MPEC and the ESCO in business strategy development, energy auditing, measurement and verification of savings, and legal aspects of performance contracting.

Strategic choices: The district heating sector needs to substantially improve its financial performance in order to provide an adequate return on capital to attract investments and make district heating enterprises attractive for privatization. From a sector perspective, the Bank is continuing its policy dialogue with the government to support sector policy development, including bringing about accounting and auditing improvements and tariff regulations that are conducive to private sector participation while meeting the government's social objectives in the sector. From a project perspective, the Bank is helping MPEC finance its modernization program during the transition period (when real tariff increases are unlikely) and improve its financial performance to a level sufficient for private or commercial financing.

The project aims to address the major barriers to energy efficiency, including the following:

- *Insufficient access to project financing*: The ESCO will act as a commercial company engaged in self-sustaining energy efficiency investments, thereby demonstrating the viability of relying on guaranteed savings in operating costs to pay back its investments and the loans of commercial banks.
- *Lack of information about the financing aspects*: The ESCO will seek to increase energy efficiency in the Krakow region by creating awareness about energy-saving opportunities. These efforts may encourage other contractors to become more active in implementing similar projects and lead to the creation of other ESCOs.
- *Lack of confidence that savings will accrue*: The ESCO will demonstrate the viability of energy management actions by bringing together the experience of all relevant players and assuming implementation and financing risks for its clients in its initial projects.
- *High transaction costs*: Demonstrating project successes will help lower transaction costs. Some ESCOs will be able to aggregate several sites for one owner under one financing agreement, opening up opportunities that otherwise would have remained elusive in uneconomic small sites.
- *Lack of an adequate institutional structure*: The project will introduce ESCO–type financing arrangements and have the utility-based ESCO become a major source of information about energy performance contracting for private and public energy users and the aggregator of demand for capital for projects.

Institutional and implementation arrangements (counterparts): MPEC coordinates implementation of the overall project and directly implements the district heating modernization component. The ESCO is responsible for implementing the ESCO component, with the help of external consultants where needed. A project implementation plan coordinates and guides the implementation efforts of MPEC and the ESCO; a project implementation agreement between MPEC and the ESCO specifies their tasks and responsibilities.

Institutional strengthening and technical assistance activities: The Bank's policy dialogue in the energy sector has concentrated on supporting the government's efforts to restructure the sector into a deregulated, competitive market. A technical assistance program provided by the Bank and by the Energy Sector Management Assistance Programme (ESMAP) is helping to complete the regulatory framework and strengthen the operational capacity of the energy regulatory authority (URE). Established in December 1997 under the new energy law, URE plays a key role in regulating tariffs for network fuels (district heating, electricity, and gas). Building on earlier ESMAP–funded support to draft the energy law and help establish URE, the follow-up ESMAP program will help URE implement the regulatory and sector reforms and advise on necessary changes to the legislation in light of experience.

Urban Environmental Aspects

The project targets urban environmental goal 3 (minimize the urban impact on natural resources at the regional and global scales). Its entire loan amount (US$15 million), as well as the proposed GEF grant (US$11 million) is allocated to addressing urban environmental issues.

The project takes an integrated approach to addressing the problems of the aging district heating infrastructure, energy inefficiency, and poor air quality in the Krakow region. It coordinates energy efficiency improvements by replacing old, inefficient equipment with new, more efficient boilers, lights, motors, and other equipment for improved hot water distribution. Energy efficiency interventions are designed to reduce the impact of emissions at the local and regional levels and the impact of greenhouse gas emissions on a global level.

The project uses two pollution reduction indicators: emission reductions of local air pollutants (sulfur dioxide, nitrogen oxides, and particulates) and the reduction in greenhouse gases (carbon dioxide) associated with the quantified energy savings (an output indicator).

Ongoing Implementation

The project is at an early stage of implementation (the loan became effective only in July 2002). Progress on development objectives has not yet been assessed. The district heating component is on track, while the ESCO component is behind schedule. Loan disbursement started immediately after loan effectiveness, with retroactive financing of US$0.9 million. Since then several contracts have been signed, bringing cumulative commitments to about US$3.174 million (21 percent of the total loan amount), which is satisfactory for the first year of project implementation. As of June 2003, loan disbursement stood at US$1.5 million (10 percent of the loan).

Consultant reviews indicate that implementation of the district heating component is progressing satisfactorily. Eight contracts relating to the district heating component have been signed.

Initial selling activity of more efficient equipment has focused on housing cooperatives, private buildings, and boiler houses for industrial plants.

Public procurement rules have made the large municipal market more difficult to enter than expected. The Bank is working separately on helping the Office of Public Procurement understand the ESCO process and possibly develop special directives and standard bidding documents to support ESCOs in Poland.

The ESCO finds itself in as good a situation as might be expected on the sales front in virgin markets, with staff learning sales techniques, and better than expected on the financing front. The key challenge will be to increase both sales and implementation capacity, while getting banks to extend larger amounts and longer maturities.

Mongolia: Improved Household Stoves in Urban Centers Project

Project Data

Project title: Improved Household Stoves in Urban Centers Project (P068108)
Sector: Energy
Region: East Asia and Pacific
Country: Mongolia
Cities and size of cities: Ulaanbaatar, 700,000; rural centers, fewer than 100,000
Sector codes: Climate change (50 percent), access to urban services for the poor (25 percent), vulnerability assessment and monitoring (25 percent)
Theme codes: State enterprise/bank restructuring and privatization (primary), other financial and private sector development (primary)
Amount of grant and total project value: US$750,000 (GEF), US$1.57 million
Fiscal year of approval: 2001
Scheduled closing date: March 31, 2005
Task Team Leader: Salvador Rivera, Senior Energy Specialist, East Asia and Pacific Energy and Mining Sector Department

Project Profile

Development objectives: This project has three objectives. It aims to reduce coal fuel consumption—and corresponding carbon dioxide emissions and levels of indoor and outdoor air pollution—in the tradition housing (*ger*) areas of Ulaanbaatar in a sustained way. It aims to facilitate the creation of a market-based institutional delivery system for establishing reliable manufacturers of efficient indoor coal stoves and developing small energy service provider companies. Also, it aims to replicate project benefits to other areas in Mongolia, particularly in rural centers.

Benefits and target population: *Ger* areas are found primarily around built-up urban areas. Dwellings in these areas are usually traditional felt tents, although they may include wooden houses, and in both such dwelling types coal-fired stoves are used. The inhabitants of *ger* areas in Ulaanbaatar and other centers will benefit through savings on fuel purchases and through improved indoor air quality. The urban population at large will benefit from improvements in ambient air quality. Energy service providers will gain from skills and business training.

Successful implementation of the project could cause overall annual coal consumption in *gers* to fall 30 percent after four years and up to 40 percent subsequently—the equivalent of 10 percent of families' annual income, with a payback period of four months for the individual investment. During the first three years, most of the low-income consumers, or about two-thirds of the population in the *ger* areas, are expected to have improvement kits installed in their traditional stoves.

The key assumption underlying the project is that there is considerable latent demand for improved stoves and stove improvements that can be met by supplying goods and services through this project. It is also assumed that households will opt for improved stoves if critical information and necessary services are made available to them.

Project description (components): The project includes five components:

- *Social marketing and increased awareness*: Production and dissemination of information on the benefits of improved stoves, the nature and size of the market, and credit mechanisms for facilitating project goals
- *Quality assurance to increase consumers' trust*: Establishment of a certification process for stove manufacturers and stove improvements, and upgrading equipment for testing improved stoves and stove improvements
- *Capacity building*: Training technicians, and providing technical assistance and skills training in evaluating new stove improvements
- *New product facility*: Evaluation and dissemination of new technical and institutional options to reduce high initial transaction costs to consumers
- *Monitoring and evaluating:* Evaluation of project's implementation progress and achievements

Strategic choices: Mongolia has one of the highest levels of greenhouse gas emissions per capita and greenhouse gas emissions per dollar of GDP in the world. During the long, bitterly cold winter, smoke sits above its towns. Air pollution is the leading cause of respiratory complaints and diseases and a major contributor to child and adult morbidity.

The primary sources of carbon dioxide emissions and air pollution are the 70,000 coal-fired urban stoves concentrated in the poor *ger* districts of Ulaanbaatar, where about 300,000 of the city's 700,000 people (43 percent) live; the combined heat and power stations; and more than 200 heat-only boilers that provide heat to areas not served by the central heating grid. Coal-fired urban stoves are estimated to contribute 30–65 percent of Ulaanbaatar's air pollution. Indoor cooking stoves consume about 350,000 tons of coal a year, with annual emissions of about half a million tons of carbon dioxide.

Improvement of household stoves was identified as a high-priority action in the 1995 National Environmental Action Plan. The government is trying to rehabilitate combined heat and power stations with support from the Asian Development Bank (ADB) and bilateral agencies.

The 1998 ALGAS report, produced by ADB, GEF, and the United Nations Development Programme (UNDP), identified improvements in coal stove efficiency as one of the 14 options for mitigating greenhouse gas emissions in the energy sector. Stove improvements ranked fourth in terms of potential for reducing carbon dioxide emissions and sixth in terms of cost effectiveness. The combined ranking placed them among the top three options rated high in terms of both feasibility and local benefits, namely, loss reduction in electricity and district heating systems, improvements in vehicle fuel consumption efficiency, and improvements in coal stove efficiency. Loss reduction in electricity and district heating systems has been the subject of a major government program supported by the Bank and ADB. Improvement in vehicle fuel consumption efficiency is a government priority and is included as a mechanical and vehicle emissions inspection program in the World Bank–supported Transport Development Project. Improvements in coal stove efficiency is the subject of this project.

Sociocultural issues: Buddhist beliefs run deep among the inhabitants of the *ger* district. A sociocultural issue that received attention during preparation is the impact of the widely held belief in the *golomt*, the hearth/fire spirit. The *golomt* is the highest being in the household. It dwells within stoves, bringing peace and good luck to those within the *ger* or house. The stove occupies the center of the *ger*, whose construction begins with its mounting. Apart from its important utilitarian purposes of heat and cooking, the stove symbolizes ties with the family's ancestors. One is not allowed to stretch one's legs toward the stove, throw trash into it, or bring sharp pointed objects close to it. Desecration of the stove is a sin and an insult to the master of the house.

The *golomt* can be passed from parent to "best" child at the discretion of the parents. The decision to change to a new stove requires consideration of the *golomt*. When a new stove is installed, a *lama*, or priest, takes ashes from the old one to place in the new one and prays that the *golomt* will reside in the new stove and bring blessings on the family as before. The reason there is no significant market for second-hand stoves is because a buyer would not know about the *golomt* of the previous owner.

The work of the team preparing the project's social marketing component included consideration of the *golomt*, and the component will both build on and be sensitive to the constraints ("desecration" of the stove during installation of kits) and opportunities (having the project activities viewed as beneficial and respectful to the *golomt*). As part of the consultation process during project preparation, the project team benefited from the participation of the Supreme Lama as advisor on aspects related to the handling of fire and ashes by technicians. The Mongolian Women's Federation has also been involved with most aspects of project preparation. Through its good contacts with *khoroo* (subdistrict) chairmen, it has helped stove manufacturers conduct in situ trials of stoves.

Other sociocultural issues were brought to the attention of the stove testers and designers during the survey work. These include householders' need to be able to see the fire and to be able to feel the heat of the stove directly from the side of the stove. These considerations were incorporated into project design.

Institutional and implementation arrangements (counterparts): The Ministry of Nature and Environment is the executing agency, through a project implementation unit. It is implementing the project in partnership with the Ulaanbaatar municipality. The ministry has designated one of its own staff as part-time project coordinator. The project coordinator reports to a steering committee chaired by the State Secretary at the Ministry of Nature and Environment and comprising stakeholder representatives, including the municipal government.

The project also funds a full-time project manager, housed at the Ministry of Nature and Environment; a part-time accountant; and other staff to deal with day-to-day management. Project execution is being carried out, to a large extent, under contracts to local NGOs with extensive experience and good track records implementing development projects in the *ger* areas.

Institutional strengthening and technical assistance activities: The project supports the evaluation, testing, and distribution of improved stoves and the development of institutional delivery systems for disseminating improved inexpensive summer woodstoves for cooking; briquettes (supported by UNDP); and new, improved stoves, kits, and best practices for saving coal and fuel wood. It helps stove manufacturers prepare business plans to finance expansion of workshop facilities to expand production capacity of improved stoves and stove improvements. Two manufacturers have already conducted discussions with local small- and medium-size enterprises to provide US$150,000 to finance the expansion of their workshops. The project also supports follow-up surveys to measure the acceptability of new products by consumers.

To reduce high initial transaction costs to consumers, the project helps the Stove Manufacturing Association organize exhibits and develop open market centers at stove selling centers in Ulaanbaatar; trains personnel in and otherwise supports the launching of open market centers as initial retailing delivery systems, including organization of initial centers; and facilitates technical assistance supported by a US$500,000 grant from the Japan International Cooperation Agency to supply steel for stove manufacturers at competitive market prices.

Urban Environmental Aspects

The project targets urban environmental goals 1 (protect and enhance environmental health in urban areas), 2 (protect water, soil, and air quality in urban areas from contamination and pollution), and 3 (minimize the urban impact on natural resources at the regional and global scales). Its entire grant amount (US$750,000) is allocated to addressing urban environmental issues.

The project integrates different urban environmental goals on local and global scales, such as reducing indoor and outdoor pollution, coal fuel consumption, and greenhouse gas emissions in *ger* areas in Ulaanbaatar and other settlements.

The project uses a pollution reduction indicator (reduction in carbon dioxide emissions from household stoves) and proxy operational indicators, which include the adoption by households of improved stoves and best practices by about 40,000 households, establishment of at least two profitable manufacturers of stove improvements and 20–40 small service providers to retrofit traditional stoves with improved kits, and the adoption of improved stoves in rural centers.

Ongoing Implementation

The project has achieved its original goals of raising awareness among consumers in the Ulaanbaatar area about options for reducing coal consumption, introducing quality control standards certification, increasing the availability of improved stoves, and establishing distribution centers in *ger* areas. A parallel government-sponsored program supports the manufacturing of about 8,000 improved stoves, which the project is helping to distribute.

A mid-term project review is planned for 2004 to address areas in which further work and realignment are required. The project aims to improve institutional implementation arrangements, with local stakeholders— including NGOs, the municipality, and local artisans—becoming the driving force during implementation, as current arrangements rely too much on centralized government implementation. The new emphasis will encourage supporting small artisans in the production of improved stoves and small service companies that introduce improved but lower-cost heating stoves and improved traditional stoves. The project will also ensure that the distribution becomes the prerogative of market operators rather than of the project implementation unit.

China: Guangzhou City Center Transport Project

Project Data

Project title: Guangzhou City Center Transport Project (P003614)
Sector: Transport
Region: East Asia and Pacific
Country: China
City and size of city: Guangzhou, 5.28 million
Sector codes: Roads and highways (75 percent), general transportation sector (25 percent)
Theme codes: Access to urban services for the poor (primary), municipal governance and institution building (primary), pollution management and environmental health (secondary)
Amount of loan and total project value: US$180 million, US$600 million
Fiscal year of approval: May 29, 1998
Scheduled closing date: December 31, 2004
Task Team Leader: Yan Zong, Transport Specialist, East Asia and Pacific Transport Sector Unit

Project Profile

Development objectives: This project aims to improve the accessibility of the city center of Guangzhou by promoting the efficient use of the urban transport system in an environmentally sustainable way.

Benefits and target population: The project is expected to reduce transport bottlenecks that slow socioeconomic development and reduce passenger and freight transport costs, lowering the price of goods and facilitating the marketing of products. The traveling public as well as the commercial and industrial producers will benefit directly through improved access to, from, and within the commercial center of Guangzhou. Public transport passengers and nonmotorized road users are expected to benefit from bus, bicycle, and pedestrian segregation and channelization facilities.

The project is designed to achieve more effective management and sustainable maintenance of road assets, including better utilization of existing road capacity, improved value for public money spent on roads, and a better fit between road maintenance activities and municipal budget allocations. The project is expected to contribute to improved health and quality of life for the citizens and users of Guangzhou's city center by reducing motor vehicle emissions and air pollution.

Project description (components): The key project components and their subcomponents include the following:

- *Inner ring road and Guangfo radial road*: Land acquisition and resettlement, viaduct and road construction, other works, materials, and construction management and supervision
- *Traffic management and safety*: Traffic management, traffic signs and signals, road safety, Guangzhou inner ring road traffic monitoring and management, parking control, and project management
- *Public transport*: Institutional reform, maintenance depot, public transport equipment, bus demonstration program, and project management
- *Vehicle pollution control*: Introduction of unleaded gasoline, a vehicle inspection and maintenance program, an automated motor vehicle pollution monitoring system, Guangzhou vehicle emission research center, and project management
- *Road maintenance*: Equipment, road maintenance system, and project management
- *Technical assistance*: Strengthening the Guangzhou inner ring road, environment protection, traffic management and safety, public transport improvement, motor vehicle pollution control, road maintenance, resettlement, transport planning and traffic engineering, and the Guangzhou city center transport project office

Institutional and implementation arrangements: The Guangzhou municipal government is the executing agency for the project. A project leading group, composed of the management of project implementing agencies and headed by a vice-mayor of the Guangzhou municipal government, has overall responsibility for project coordination. The project office is responsible to the project leading group for the organization and management of project implementation. The principal implementing agency is the Guangzhou City Center Transport Construction Company, a new entity established to manage the construction and implementation of the Guangzhou inner ring road.

Strategic choices: No single project can address all the transport sector issues found in Guangzhou, some of which require provincial or even national policy attention (for example, industrial policy affecting the automotive industry). Project choices were based on consideration of the issues that the Guangzhou municipality is already addressing, the most pressing needs, and the areas in which the Bank can best offer assistance.

The project includes components that address the following transport sector issues within the context of local priorities and development plans:

- supply of new infrastructure to alleviate congestion and provide needed new capacity
- traffic management based on functional hierarchy of roads, channelization, and operational and regulatory aspects
- public transport operational efficiency
- inadequacies in road maintenance management
- mitigation of motor vehicle air pollution
- institutional strengthening and capacity building

Institutional strengthening and technical assistance activities: This component aims to strengthen institutional capacity for planning, administering, and managing public programs by supporting the following:

- domestic training, including lectures, training courses, study tours, and on-site training
- international training, including study tours, university training, and on-site training
- domestic and foreign consulting services
- research, development, and study of various topics
- software and communications and transport equipment

Urban Environmental Aspects

The project targets urban environmental goal 2 (protect water, soil, and air quality in urban areas from contamination and pollution). It aims to reduce the level of air pollution by introducing traffic management measures and improving coordination among responsible agencies. The 26.7 kilometers of urban road development is expected to ease long-term traffic congestion in the city center, improve the quality of urban life, and stimulate economic development. To address urban environmental issues, a portion of the loan is allocated to a motor vehicle emission control component. Funds from the project are also allocated to preparing an environmental action plan that supports specific mitigation measures for noise control, construction impacts control, project vicinity landscaping, and environmental supervision.

The main indicators include an improved level of service and reduced congestion on the city center road network, increased throughput of public transport corridors within the city center, reduction in relative levels of mobile-source air pollution, reduction in the number of accidents per capita, and improved effectiveness and efficiency of the road maintenance program.

Ongoing Implementation

Throughout implementation the project has been rated satisfactory in terms of achievement of development objectives and implementation progress. A project restructuring was completed in April 2003. The project was expanded to US$600 million from the original US$586.1 million, while the loan size was reduced from US$200 million to US$180 million. The main amendments are the addition of the Guangfo radial road, the reallocation of project components, the cancellation of US$20 million in lending, and the extension of the loan to December 31, 2004.

The environmental benefits are beginning to emerge. Carbon monoxide levels have fallen from a baseline of 2.54 mg/m^3 throughout the city and 3.02 mg/m^3 in the city center to a citywide average of 2.29 mg/m^3. Nitrogen oxide levels have fallen from a baseline of 0.139 mg/m^3 throughout the city and 0.162 mg/m^3 in the city center to a citywide average of 0.113 mg/m^3. The level of total suspended particulates (TSP) has fallen from a citywide baseline of 0.213 mg/m^3 to 0.150 mg/m^3.

Institutional strengthening with a direct bearing on the urban environment has included recruitment of permanent environmental staff in the Guangzhou municipal government; a joint effort by the Guangzhou municipal government, the Environment Protection Bureau, the Environmental Monitoring Center, the Planning Bureau, the Traffic Management Bureau, and the traffic police to develop motor vehicle emission control strategies and noise mitigation measures; establishment of a permanent environmental hotline; and the building of capability of the local environmental assessment team.

Design for a Guangzhou vehicle emission research center has been completed, and bidding for contractors and equipment suppliers is proceeding. The automatic air quality and noise monitoring system upgrading is also in the bidding stage. About 6.5 kilometers of noise barriers—much more than the 3.6 kilometers planned in the environmental action plan—have been erected along sensitive sections of the project roads. Double-glazed windows and air conditioning have been installed in two schools as a pilot project and will be erected in other impacted sensitive areas. The open space in the vicinity of the project roads has been landscaped as planned.

Several changes were introduced during design, construction, and operation:

• The least problematic road alignments were selected.

- Porous asphalt was used extensively to create quieter road surfaces.
- Longer prefabricated structures were used to minimize the number of joints.
- Noise barriers were used at road sections near sensitive receptors.
- Changes were made to the motor vehicle emission control component, including changes to strategy development, the motor vehicle emission research center, the inspection and maintenance program, and the city-wide automatic air quality monitoring system.

Several difficulties have been encountered so far in project implementation. These difficulties include the lack of environmental awareness of the municipal government, design teams, contractors, and the general public; disagreement between the Bank and the environmental assessment team on interpreting and implementing regulatory standards, such as noise standards; and weak enforcement of environmental standards and mitigation measures.

Bibliography

Abuyuan, Alethea M.T. 2002. "Private Sector Development and the Environment: An Analysis of the Bank Privatization Portfolio." Environment Strategy Paper No. 5. World Bank, Washington, D.C.

Bartone, Carl. 2001. "Urban Environmental Priorities." Environment Strategy Background Paper. World Bank, Washington, D.C.

Bartone, Carl, Janis Bernstein, Josef Leitmann, and Jochen Eigen. 1994. "Toward Environmental Strategies for Cities: Policy Considerations for Urban Environmental Management in Developing Countries." Urban Management Program Paper No. 18. World Bank, Washington D.C.

Bernstein, Janis D. 1991. "Alternative Approaches to Pollution Control and Waste Management: Regulatory and Economic Instruments." Urban Management Program Paper No. 3. World Bank, Washington, D.C.

———. 1995. *The Urban Challenge in National Environmental Strategies.* Environmental Management Series Paper No. 012. World Bank, Washington, D.C.

Bigio, Anthony G. 2001. *Clear Air Initiative in Latin American Cities: Progress Report 2001.* Washington, D.C.: World Bank.

———. 2003. "Cities and Climate Change." In Alcira Kreimer, Margaret Arnold, and Anne Carlin, eds. *Building Safer Cities: The Future of Disaster Risk.* Washington, D.C.: World Bank.

Bigio, Anthony G., and Bharat Dahiya. 2003. "World Bank Investments for the Urban Environment." Environment Strategy Note No. 8. World Bank, Environment Department, Washington, D.C.

Bolt, Katherine. 2002. "The Millennium Development Goals and the Environment." In *Environment Matters at the World Bank: Annual Review.* Washington, D.C.: World Bank.

Campbell, Tim. 1989. "Environmental Dilemmas and the Urban Poor." In H. Jeffrey Leonard, ed. *Environment and the Poor: Development Strategies for a Common Agenda.* New Brunswick, N.J.: Transactions Books.

Dahiya, Bharat. 1999. "World Bank Lending for the Urban Environment: A Portfolio Analysis." Urban Development Division Study. World Bank, Washington, D.C. Processed.

————. 2001. *Whither Urban Governance? Self-Help Civil Society, Environmental Services and Political Conflicts*. PhD thesis, Sidney Sussex College, University of Cambridge.

————. 2003a. "Hard Struggle and Soft Gains: Environmental Management, Civil Society, and Governance in Pammal, South India." *Environment and Urbanization* 15(1): 91–100.

————. 2003b. "Peri-Urban Environments and Community-Driven Development: Chennai, India." *Cities* 20(5):341–52.

Dahiya, Bharat, and Cedric Pugh. 2000. "The Localization of Agenda 21 and the Sustainable Cities Programme." In Cedric Pugh, ed. *Sustainable Cities in Developing Countries: Theory and Practice at the Millennium*. London: Earthscan.

Foster, Stephen, Adrian Lawrence, and Brian Morris. 1998. "Groundwater in Urban Development: Assessing Management Needs and Formulating Policy Strategies." World Bank Technical Paper No. 390. Washington, D.C.

Freeman, Paul K., Leslie A. Martin, Reinhard Mechler, and Koko Warner. 2002. "Catastrophes and Development: Integrating Natural Catastrophes into Development Planning." Disaster Risk Management Working Paper Series No. 4. World Bank, Washington, D.C.

Gochenour, Carolyn. 2001. "District Energy Trends, Issues, and Opportunities: The Role of the World Bank." World Bank Technical Paper No. 493. Washington, D.C.

Hardoy, Jorge Enrique, Diana Mitlin, and David Satterthwaite. 2001. *Environmental Problems in an Urbanizing World: Finding Solutions in Africa, Asia, and Latin America*. London: Earthscan.

Hewawasam, Indu. 2002. *Managing the Marine and Coastal Environment of Sub-Saharan Africa: Strategic Directions for Sustainable Development*. Washington, D.C.: World Bank.

Hughes, Gordon, Kseniya Lvovsky, and Meghan Dunleavy. 2001. *Environmental Health in India: Priorities in Andhra Pradesh*. South Asia Environment and Social Development Unit, Washington, D.C. : World Bank.

Hunt, Caroline, Sandy Cairncross, Manish Dubey, Peter Kolsky, Simon Lewin, Rajashi Mukherjee, V. Ramaswamy, Aromar Rev, Carolyn Stephens, and the Sustainable Indicators Team. 1999. "Community-Based Environmental Health Indicators: A Useful Tool in Facilitating Dialogue between Communities and Planners?" *Urban Health and Development Bulletin* 2(2):82–90.

Karekezi, Stephen, Lugard Majoro, and Todd Johnson. 2003. *Climate Change Mitigation in the Urban Transport Sector: Priorities for the World Bank*. Washington, D.C.: World Bank.

Kessides, Christine. 1997. "World Bank Experience with the Provision of Infrastructure Services for the Urban Poor: Preliminary Identification and Review of Best Practices." Paper No. TWU-OR8. World Bank, Washington, D.C.

Kojima, Masami, Carter Brandon, and Jitendra Shah. 2000. *Improving Urban Air Quality in South Asia by Reducing Emissions from Two-Stroke Engine Vehicles*. Washington, D.C.: World Bank, South Asia Environment Unit.

Kojima, Masami, and Magda Lovei. 2001. "Urban Air Quality Management: Coordinating Transport, Environment, and Energy Policies in Developing Countries." Pollution Management Series, Technical Paper No. 508. World Bank, Washington, D.C.

Kolev, Alexandre, and Rosanna Nitti. 2001. *Constructing Multi-Sector Monitoring and Evaluation Indicators for Poverty-Focused Interventions: The Case of Infrastructure*. Washington, D.C.: World Bank, Infrastructure Group.

Kreimer, Alcira, and Mohan Munasinghe. 1991. "Managing Environmental Degradation and Natural Disasters: An Overview." In Alcira Kreimer and Mohan Munasinghe, eds. *Managing Natural Disasters and the Environment*. Washington, D.C.: World Bank.

Kreimer, Alcira, Thereza Lobo, Braz Menezes, Mohan Munasinghe, and Ronald Parker, eds. 1993. "Toward a Sustainable Urban Environment: The Rio de Janeiro Study." World Bank Discussion Paper 195. Washington, D.C.

Leitmann, Josef. 1994a. *Rapid Environmental Assessment: Lessons from Countries in the Developing World. Vol. 1, Methodology and Findings*. Washington, D.C.: World Bank, Urban Management Program.

———. 1994b. *Rapid Environmental Assessment: Lessons from Countries in the Developing World. Vol. 2, Tools and Outputs*. Washington, D.C.: World Bank, Urban Management Program.

———. 1994c. "The World Bank and the Brown Agenda: Evolution of a Revolution." *Third World Planning Review* 16(2):117–127.

———. 1999. *Sustaining Cities: Environmental Planning and Management in Urban Design*. New York: McGraw-Hill.

Linares, Carlos A. 2003. *Institutions and the Urban Environment in Developing Countries: Challenges, Trends, and Transitions*. New Haven, Conn.: Yale School of Forestry and Environmental Studies.

Lovei, Magda, and Bradford S. Gentry. 2002. "The Environmental Implications of Privatization: Lessons for Developing Countries." Discussion Paper No. 426. World Bank, Washington, D.C.

Lvovsky, Kseniya. 2001. *Health and Environment*. Environment Strategy Paper No. 1. World Bank, Washington, D.C.

Lvovski, Kseniya, Gordon Hughes, David Maddison, Bart Ostro, and David Pearce. 2000. "Environmental Costs of Fossil Fuels: A Rapid Assessment Method with Application to Six Cities." Pollution Management Series, Paper No. 78. World Bank, Washington, D.C.

McGranahan, Gordon. 1995. "Health, Poverty, and the Environment: Lessons from a Three-City Study." In Ismail Serageldin, Michael A. Cohen, and K. C. Sivaramakrishnan, eds. *The Human Face of the Urban Environment*. Environmentally Sustainable Development Occasional Paper 6. Washington, D.C.: World Bank.

McGranahan, Gordon, and Frank Murray, eds. 2003. *Air Pollution and Health in Rapidly Developing Countries*. London: Earthscan

Munasinghe, Mohan. 1993. "Environmental Economics and Sustainable Development." World Bank Environment Paper No. 3. Washington, D.C.

Paul, Samuel. 1991. "Accountability in Public Services: Exit, Voice, and Capture." Policy, Research, and External Affairs Working Paper 614. World Bank, Washington, D.C.

Pugh, Cedric, ed. 1996. *Sustainability, the Environment and Urbanization*. London: Earthscan.

————. 2000. ed. *Sustainable Cities in Developing Countries: Theory and Practice at the Millennium*. London: Earthscan.

Reuben, William, Tania Barron, and Carmen Monico. 2002. *Social Development Update: Monitoring Civic Engagement in Bank Lending and Policy Instruments*. Washington, D.C.: World Bank, Environmentally and Socially Sustainable Department.

Sarin, Prem, and Tee Guidotti. 2002. *Evaluation of Environmental Health Indictors in World Bank Projects: A Report on the Potential Use of Health Indicators in Sustainable Development Projects*. Washington, D.C.: George Washington University Medical Center, Department of Environmental and Occupational Health.

Segnestam, Lisa. 1999. "Environmental Performance Indicators: A Second Edition Note." Environmental Economics Series Paper No. 71. World Bank, Washington, D.C.

Serageldin, Ismail, Michael A. Cohen, and K. C. Sivaramakrishnan, eds. 1995. "The Human Face of the Urban Environment." Environmentally Sustainable Development Occasional Paper 6. World Bank, Washington, D.C.

Shyamsundar, Priya. 2002. "Poverty: Environment Indicators." Environmental Economics Series Paper No. 84. World Bank, Washington, D.C.

Shin, Euisoon, Maynard Hufschmidt, Yok-shiu Lee, James E. Nickum, and Chieko Umetsu, with Regina Gregory. 1997. "Valuating the Economic Impacts of Urban Environmental Problems: Asian Cities." Urban Management Program Working Paper 13. World Bank, Washington, D.C.

Sustainable Cities Programme. 2000. "City Experiences in Improving the Urban Environment: A Snapshot of Six City Initiatives in Africa, 1999." Urban Environment, Sustainable Cities Programme Working Paper No. 1. United Nations Centre for Human Settlements, Nairobi.

————. 2001. "Implementation and Replication of the Sustainable Cities Programme Process at City and National Level: Case Studies from Nine

Cities." Urban Environment Unit, Sustainable Cities Programme Working Paper No. 2. United Nations Centre for Human Settlements, Nairobi.

UNCHS (United Nations Centre for Human Settlements). 2001. *Cities in a Globalizing World: Global Report on Human Settlements 2001*. London: Earthscan.

————. 1997b. *The Istanbul Declaration and Habitat Agenda*. Nairobi.

United Nations. 1993. *Report of the United Nations Conference of Environment and Development*. New York: United Nations.

United Nations Human Settlements Programme. 2003a. *The Challenge of Slums: Global Report on Human Settlements*. London: Earthscan.

————. 2003b. *Water and Sanitation in the World's Cities: Local Action for Global Goals*. London: Earthscan.

Venard, J. L. 1995. *Urban Planning and Environment in Sub-Saharan Africa*. Building Blocks for AFRICA 2025 Paper No. 5. World Bank, Africa Technical Department, Environmentally Sustainable Development Division, Washington, D.C.

Von Schirnding, Yasmin, Carlos Corvalan, and Greg Goldstein. 1999. "Indicators for Environment, Health, and Development." *Urban Health and Development Bulletin* 2(2):76–81.

Walter, Jonathan, ed. 2002. *World Disasters Report: Focus on Reducing Risk*. Geneva: International Federation of the Red Cross and Red Crescent Societies.

World Bank. 1991. *Urban Policy and Economic Development: An Agenda for the 1990s*. World Bank, Washington, D.C.

————. 1992. *Governance and Development*. World Bank, Washington, D.C.

————. 1995a. *Better Urban Services: Finding the Right Incentives*. Development in Practice Series. World Bank, Washington, D.C.

————. 1995b. *Mainstreaming the Environment: The World Bank Group and the Environment Since the Rio Earth Summit*. World Bank, Washington, D.C.

————. 1996. *Livable Cities for the 21st Century*. Directions in Development Series. World Bank, Washington, D.C.

————. 1998. *Brazil: Managing Pollution Problems: The Brown Environmental Agenda*. Latin America and Caribbean Region, Environmentally and Socially Sustainable Development Sector Management Unit, World Bank, Washington, D.C.

————. 1999a. *Entering the 21st Century: World Development Report 1999/2000*. World Bank, Washington, D.C.

————. 1999b. *Pollution Prevention and Abatement Handbook 1998: Toward Cleaner Production*. World Bank, Washington, D.C.

————. 1999c. *A Strategic View of Urban and Local Government Issues: Implications for the Bank*. World Bank, Washington, D.C.

————. 2000a. *Cities in Transition: The World Bank Urban and Local Government Strategy*. World Bank, Washington, D.C.

————. 2000b. *Greening Industry: New Roles for Communities, Markets, and Governments*. New York: Oxford University Press.

————. 2001a. *Cleaner Transport Fuels for Cleaner Air in Central Asia and the Caucasus*. Report 242/01. Energy Sector Management Assistance Programme, World Bank, Washington, D.C.

————. 2001b. *Making Sustainable Commitments: An Environment Strategy for the World Bank*. World Bank, Washington, D.C.

————. 2002a. *Cities on the Move: A World Bank Urban Transport Strategy Review*. World Bank, Washington, D.C.

————. 2002b. *Energy and the Environment: Energy and Development Report 2001*. Energy and Mining Sector Board/Energy Sector Management Assistance Programme. World Bank, Washington, D.C.

————. 2002c. *Improving the Lives of the Poor through Investment in Cities: An Update on the Performance of the World Bank's Urban Portfolio*. Washington, D.C.: World Bank, Operations Evaluation Department.

————. 2002d. *Mongolia: Improved Space Heating Stoves for Ulaanbaatar*. Report 254/02. Energy Sector Management Assistance Programme, World Bank, Washington, D.C.

————. 2002e. *Monitoring and Evaluation: Some Tools, Methods, and Approaches*. Washington, D.C.: World Bank, Operations Evaluation Department.

————. 2002f. *The World Bank and Agenda 21*. Washington, D.C.

World Resources Institute, United Nations Development Programme, United Nations Environment Programme, and the World Bank. 1996. *World Resources 1996–97: A Guide to the Global Environment: The Urban Environment*. New York: Oxford University Press.

Index

air quality, *see* water, soil, and air quality (project goal 2)

Algeria, Industrial Pollution Control Project, 32, 108–113

Bombay Sewage Disposal Project (India), 28, 73–78

brown agenda, xiv, 3, 8, 59–60

Business Warehouse, 9

Caracas Slum-Upgrading Project (Venezuela), 30, 91–96

Cartagena Water Supply, Sewerage, and Environmental Management Project (Nicaragua), 28, 79–84

case studies, xviii–xix, 3–4, 63–64

  Bombay Sewage Disposal Project (India), 28, 73–78

  Caracas Slum-Upgrading Project (Venezuela), 30, 91–96

  Cartagena Water Supply, Sewerage, and Environmental Management Project (Nicaragua), 28, 79–84

  Energy sector, 33–34

  Environment sector, 32

  Transport sector, 35

  Urban Development sector, 29–30

  Water and Sanitation sector, 27–28

China

  Guangzhou City Center Transport Project, 35, 133–137

  Liaoning Environmental Project, 28, 67–72

city size, xvi–xvii, 36–40, *see also* tables, charts, and figures

  emphasis on small cities, xvii, 36–37

  regional variations, 37–38

  sector contributions, 39, 40

  strengths and weaknesses of Portfolio, 57

  urban environmental goals, 38

  World Bank projects analyzed by, 36–37, 39–40

civil society, xvii, 42–44

climate change, *see* natural disasters and climate change (project goal 4)

Earth Summit (United Nations Conference on Environment and Development), 1992, xiv, 5

Energy sector, 32–34

Environment sector, 31–32